HUMAN RESOURCE MANAGEMENT STUDY GAMES

Certification Prep and Refresher

Gundars Kaupins

University Press of America,® Inc.
Lanham · Boulder · New York · Toronto · Plymouth, UK

4501 Forbes Boulevard
Suite 200
Lanham, Maryland 20706
UPA Acquisitions Department (301) 459-3366

10 Thornbury Road
Plymouth PL6 7PP
United Kingdom

Printed in the United States of America
British Library Cataloging in Publication Information Available

Library of Congress Control Number: 2014936786
ISBN: 978-0-7618-6378-6 (paperback : alk. paper)
eISBN: 978-0-7618-6379-3

™ The paper used in this publication meets the minimum requirements of American National Standard for Information Sciences—Permanence of Paper for Printed Library Materials, ANSI Z39.48-1992

Dedications

To my wonderful, loving, wise, and creative wife Debby Queen, son, Kyle Kaupins, daughter Amanda Queen, and international "daughter" Nato Peikrishvilli. To my great parents, Alfred and Skaidrite Kaupins.

Contents

Foreword

If you are wondering if this book about HR Games will really help you learn the complexities of the human resource field, I can assure you that the author, Dr. Gundars (Gundy) Kaupins, has done that effectively for over 9 years at the Boise State Center for Professional Development.

People come to the Boise State Center for Professional Development to learn what it takes to both launch and advance in their careers. We require that the instructors of our courses are both knowledgeable and skilled in design learning strategies that are effective for adults. Gundy has brought his experience in teaching human resources and writing HR certification test question to facilitate both foundational and PHR/SPHR certification courses.

Despite the complexity and scope of the materials, even those who were really concerned that their experience was too limited complete the course with reports that they learned more than they anticipated. Consistently, they tell us that the varied activities truly engaged them and made the time fly. The effectiveness of learning games is demonstrated by the high success rate they report on the exams. It is these same "games" which are now described in this book.

Gaining and maintaining mastery of the primarily terms, laws and research results can be a challenge both to pass certification exams and provide professional advice in the workplace. This book will be a valuable resource that you can adapt to enter new content as laws and practices evolve. Do yourself a favor, put the tools in this book to use, and advance your *game!*

Bae Emilson, MA, SPHR
Director, Boise State Center for Professional Development

Preface

Human Resource Management Study Games: Certification Prep and Refresher has several purposes. Human resource (HR) students and professionals have games they can use to help study for HR classes and certification exams. The games in this book serve as a supplement to textbooks, certification exam materials, and information found on the Web. The games assume a prior knowledge of human resources from these main sources of information. The book adds some information by organizing HR facts in new ways and providing details on laws.

HR instructors for college classes and certification exam programs can obtain ideas on how to create games to make their classes more educational and fun. The book contains four main games—Definition Matrix, Brainstorming, CREEDO, and Multiple Choice. Many varieties of these basic games can be played using the contents of the book. These games also can be created based on textbooks, certification exam materials, and information found on the Web.

Fun and learning should sneak their way in the games. Why not?

Acknowledgements

Thanks to Angela Kassis, Meghan Sorenson, Terri Allen, and Angela Magnuson who helped with the creation of some of the CREEDO games.

Chapter One

WHY PLAY GAMES?

Games can be one of the most effective methods to help students study for human resource management. Games are among the top methods of training people because they provide high knowledge retention, knowledge acquisition, and player acceptance.

Here are some other reasons to play games:

Many senses can be used (seeing, hearing, tasting, touching, smelling). People have different preferences—some are visual, some are auditory, and some are kinesthetic and like learning by doing. A visual person may focus on reading books, diagrams, and charts. An auditory person may like discussions, hear lectures, or focus on online chats. A kinesthetic person may like to do role plays and demonstrations in class. Outside of class, this person might like internships and apprenticeships.

Many games can be used. People like variety and games can provide some of that variety. Some games can allow learners to focus getting the one right answer such as quiz-related games. Other games allow learners to brainstorm a variety of topics. The games can be combined with other training methods such as lectures, role plays, webinars, etc.

Active participation is a trademark of games. Most adults would rather learn by participation than passively listen to a lecture. High pressure can be part of the games in which real prizes are given to the winners.

Personal experiences can relate to the games. The experiences can be either their life experiences or experiences that they just learned from the games.

Direct contact occurs between the instructor and the students. Human contact allows the instructor to immediately respond to any question from the students and to hopefully understand needs. If direct contact can't occur, a possible substitute is computer contact. Learners can complete simulations or answer multiple choice questions.

There are many other advantages. Games can provide *rewards* to students who have learned the most. There is often immediate *feedback* with games. Games often lead to *creativity* in which new problems and solutions are generated. Games can help learners *organize* information in narrow chunks to help memorization. Games are *fun*.

Games might not be for everyone. They are one of many study options such as reading books, following lectures, and solving case studies. Whatever works best for each person's learning style should be used.

Chapter Two

Why Study HR?

Ultimately, studying HR would improve knowledge of the field. This helps with your effectiveness as an HR manager and ultimately helps your organization achieve its strategic objectives and bottom line.

Beyond college and noncredit courses, studying HR would help students achieve certifications that can help improve employability. Below are some of the most common HR programs and certifications that should be considered.

ASSURANCE OF LEARNING

Purpose: Demonstrate HR knowledge for recent HR or HR-related college graduates.
http://www2.shrm.org/assuranceoflearning/index.html
Cost: $210 ($135 Society for HR Management (SHRM) Members)
Questions: 160 *Length of Exam:* 3 hours
Type of Questions: Multiple choice covering definitions, laws, and research results.
Eligibility: Undergraduate students and graduate students in HR or HR-related degree programs beginning as early as one year before graduation and up to one year after graduation.
Topics Covered: Training and development (12 questions), Workforce planning (40 questions), strategy (40 questions), Total rewards (20 questions), Employment law (28 questions), Employee and labor relations (20 questions)

PROFESSIONAL IN HUMAN RESOURCES (PHR)

Purpose: Show HR knowledge for the HR professional who focuses on program implementation and has a tactical/logistical orientation.
http://www.hrci.org/our-programs/our-hr-certifications/phr
Cost: $400 $350 SHRM Members
Number of Questions: 175 Length of Exam: 3 hours
Type of Questions: Multiple choice covering definitions, laws, and research results.
Eligibility: A minimum of 1 year of experience in an exempt-level (professional) HR position with a Master's degree or higher, OR
A minimum of 2 years of experience in an exempt-level (professional) HR position with a Bachelor's degree, OR
A minimum of 4 years of experience in an exempt-level (professional) HR position with a high school diploma
Topics Covered: Strategic Management 11%; Workforce Planning and Employment 24%, Human Resource Development 18%; Total Rewards 19%; Employee and Labor Relations 20%; Risk Management 8%

SENIOR PROFESSIONAL IN HUMAN RESOURCES (SPHR)

Purpose: Demonstrates HR knowledge and problem solving skills for the HR professional who focuses on the big pictures has ultimate accountability in the HR department.
http://www.hrci.org/our-programs/our-hr-certifications/sphr
Cost: $525 ($475 SHRM members)
Questions: 175 *Length of Exam:* 3 hours
Type of Questions: Multiple choice. Exam questions assume that a manager, employee, customer, or other individual walk into an HR office with a problem. They do not know any definitions, laws, or research results. It is the HR manager's role to hear their problem and to answer their problem based on knowledge of definitions, laws, and research results.
Eligibility: A minimum of 4 years of experience in an exempt-level (professional) HR position with a Master's degree or higher, OR
A minimum of 5 years of experience in an exempt-level (professional) HR position with a Bachelor's degree, OR
A minimum of 7 years of experience in an exempt-level (professional) HR position with a high school diploma
Topics Covered: Strategic Management 30%; Workforce Planning and Employment 17%; Human Resource Development 19%; Total Rewards 13%; Employee and Labor Relations 14%; Risk Management 7%

SELECTED OTHER CERTIFICATIONS

From the Society for Human Resource Management (SPHR):

Global Professional in Human Resources (GPHR)
Demonstrates the mastery of cross-border HR responsibilities.
http://www.hrci.org/our-programs/our-hr-certifications/gphr

Human Resource Management Professional (HRMP)
Demonstrates mastery of generally accepted HR principles in strategy and policy development as well as service delivery independent of geographic region.
http://www.hrci.org/our-programs/our-hr-certifications/hrmp

Human Resource Business Professional (HRBP): Purpose: Demonstrates mastery of generally accepted technical and operational HR principles. Independent of geographic region.
http://www.hrci.org/our-programs/our-hr-certifications/hrbp

From WorldAtWork:

Certified Compensation Professional (CCP)
Demonstrates essential knowledge about integrating compensation programs with business strategy and related activities.
http://www.worldatworksociety.org/society/certification/html/certification-ccp-us.jsp

Certified Benefits Professional (CBP)
Signifies the essential U.S. specific knowledge about integrating benefits programs with business strategy and related activities.
http://www.worldatworksociety.org/certification/html/certification-cbp-us.jsp

Global Remuneration Professional (GRP)
Shows the knowledge, skills and training needed to design, manage and deliver global rewards programs.
http://www.worldatworksociety.org/certification/html/certification-grp.jsp

Work-Life Certified Professional (WLCP)
Demonstrates that you have the knowledge and critical skills to design, administer and manage work-life programs.
http://www.worldatworksociety.org/certification/html/certification-wlcp.jsp

From the American Society for Training and Development (ASTD):

Certified Professional in Learning and Performance
Provides a way for workplace learning and performance professionals to prove their value to employers and to be confident about their knowledge of the field.
http://www.astd.org/Certification

From the International Public Management Association for Human Resources (IPMA-HR):

IPMA-HR Certified Professional (IPMA-CP)
Demonstrates competency in public sector HR.
http://ipma-hr.org/professional-development/certification

Chapter Three

Definition Matrix Games

PURPOSE

Be able to know terms and laws. The terminology is useful for helping pass human resource courses and certification exams.

WAYS TO PLAY

Written Matrix

One Player: Write down all of the answers to the chosen definition matrix. Check answers on the appropriate answer matrix in the next few pages. Add a point for each answer that is correct and take away a point for each answer that is incorrect. Total your score.

Two or More Players: All players look at a matrix and write down their answers. Add a point for each answer that is correct and take away a point for each answer that is incorrect. The player with the most points wins.

Buzzer Matrix

Two or More Players: Have one person give the clues and the other person(s) provide the answers. Add a point for each question right and minus one for each question wrong. With three players, the first person to respond by buzzer, bell, or hand gets to answer the question.

Two or More Players: Create a grid from glossaries from HR textbooks and Websites.

Definition Matrix Game 1—Strategic Management

Strategic Planning	*Organization Design*	*Human Resource Auditing*	*Ethical Issues*	*Mathematics and Statistics*
A—First step, start business, existence reason	A—Structure in which regional, market, or product sections are created	A—Formal review of outcomes of human resource management functions	A—Machines used to determine truthfulness of a witness	A—Average; score divided by number in the sample
B—View of the corporation more the five years in the future	B—Structure in which it is divided into marketing, accounting, HR, finance	B—Amount of revenues over expenses	B—Act of keeping a close watch over an employee	B—Middle number; end of second quartile
C—Examples include honesty, creativity, learning, openness, and quality customer service	C—Amount of decision-making authority provided to lower levels of an organization	C—Individual involved with communicating and enforcing codes of conduct	C—Right to keep personal information a secret	C—Extreme number in a set of data, a number much higher or lower than normal
D—Objectives for three to five years in the future	D—Structure combining functional and divisional designs	D—Rate of movement of employees out of an organization	D—Hiring an individual known to commit illegal activities	D—The most frequent number in a set of data
E—Short for strengths, weaknesses, opportunities, and threats analysis	E—Fayol principle in which there should be one leader rather than multiple leaders	E—Asset turnover ratio multiplied by the profit margin on sales	E—Person who has five percent ownership in a company during the present or previous year	E—Shows how much a probability function is away from the mean

Definition Matrix Game 1—Strategic Management

Strategic Planning	*Organization Design*	*Human Resource Auditing*	*Ethical Issues*	*Mathematics and Statistics*
F—Strategies that business functions such as human resource management and finance create	F—Companies engaged in different production levels such as manufacturing and distribution	F—Knowledge gained through problem formulation, observation or experiment, and testing hypotheses	F—Exclusive ownership right in a published work created by an author	F—Relationship between two or more correlated variables
G—Detailed business unit short-term objectives	G—Companies engaged in the same production level such as one manufacturer owning another	G—Experimental and control groups and random selection of inputs	G—Conditions in which a person may unfairly benefit from an association with another organization	G—Number that indicates the degree of relationship between two variables
H—Planning involved with developing, implementing and evaluating corporate decisions to achieve objectives	H—Number of individuals who serve under a manager	H—Determining the best practices of competitors for comparison with your own organization	H—Revealing illegal corporate behavior to the government	H—Statistical analysis of variable patterns such as seasonality over time
I—Framework linking business strategies to business programs	I—Defined set of activities designed to complete a project	I—To ask people questions in order to collect data about them for analysis	I—Number of the constitutional amendment involving freedom of speech	I—Probability density function approximating a large number of random variable distributions
J—Activities designed to deploy organizational resources to implement strategies	J—Structure based on how customers are organized	J—State of being effective in bringing about results	J—Usually involving urine samples and associated with employee hiring	J—Standard deviation squared

Answer Matrix Game 1—Strategic Management

Strategic Planning	*Organization Design*	*Human Resource Auditing*	*Ethical Issues*	*Mathematics and Statistics*
A—Mission	A—Divisional structure	A—HR audit	A—Polygraphs	A—Mean
B—Vision	B—Functional structure	B—Profitability	B—Surveillance	B—Median
C—Values	C—Decentralization	C—Ombudsman or ethics officer	C—Privacy	C—Outlier
D—Long term objectives	D—Matrix structure	D—Turnover rate	D—Negligent hiring	D—Mode
E—SWOT analysis	E—Unity of command	E—Return on investment	E—Highly compensated employee	E—Standard deviation
F—Functional strategies	F—Vertical integration	F—Scientific method	F—Copyright	F—Regression
G—Action plan	G—Horizontal integration	G—Experimental design	G—Conflict of interest	G—Correlation
H—Strategic planning	H—Span of control	H—Benchmarking	H—Whistle blowing	H—Time series analysis
I—Balanced Scorecard	I—Project management	I—Survey	I—First Amendment	I—Normal distribution
J—Tactics	J—Customer structure	J—Productivity	J—Drug testing	J—Variance

Definition Matrix Game 2—Global HR

Name the Country	*Cultural Dimensions*	*International Organizations*	*People*	*Trade*
A—Kaizen (or continuous improvement)	A-Extent to which society expects power to be distributed	A—Supports international trade agreements (replaced the GATT)	A—Head of the United Nations	A—Government financial assistance to a domestic producer
B—Co-determination	B—Degree to which society is loyal to the org. or family	B—Provides economic guidelines for global organizations	B—People who move from the base company to work in another country	B—Charges against imports
C—Enterprise Union	C—Degree to which society relies on norms to reduce unpredictability	C—Contains the Security Council	C—People who come back from international work	C—Country with low income taxes
D—Exclusive bargaining representation	D—Degree to which society focuses on male leadership	D—Responsible for the Euro	D—Foreigners sent in to work at a headquarters company	D—Company hands over key to foreign client when plant operational
E—Life time employment in large orgs.	E—Degree to which society focuses on future-oriented behaviors	E—Set up to provide stability in the international monetary system	E—Any person on a global posting	E—National accounts that track both payments to and foreigner receipts

Definition Matrix Game 2—Global HR

Name the Country	*Cultural Dimensions*	*International Organizations*	*People*	*Trade*
F—French and English speaking divisions	F—Researcher of power distance, uncertainty avoidance and other dimensions	F—United Nations agency that establishes international labor standards	F—Head of an international union	F—Absence of barriers to free flow of goods between countries
G—Maquiladora—manufacturing operation in a free trade zone	G—Extent to which society is assertive towards others	G—Set up to promote economic development in world's poorest nations	G—Chief international official in the U. S. Cabinet	G—The rate at which one currency is converted to another currency
H—Labor Party, Conservative Party	H—Distinct ways that people live differently	H—Attempts to provide uniform accounting standards across countries	H—Persona non grata	H—Limit on the quantity of goods that can be imported from a country
I—Communist leaders of economic dynamo	I—Country that scores highest on Individualism	I—Judicial branch of the United Nations	I—Jus inter gentes	I—Free trade area between Canada, Mexico and the U. S.
J—Samsung	J—European region that scores highest on feminism	J—Corporation that produces and sells goods in multiple countries	J—Jus soli	J—Trade agreement between U. S. and Costa Rica et. al.

Answer Matrix Game 2—Global HR

Name the Country	*Cultural Dimensions*	*International Organizations and Agreements*	*People*	*Trade*
A—Japan	A—Power Distance	A—World Trade Organization (WTO)	A—Secretary General	A—Subsidy
B—Germany	B—Collectivism	B—Org. for Economic Coop. And Development (OECD)	B—Expatriates	B—Tariffs
C—Japan	C—Uncertainty Avoidance	C—United Nations (UN)	C—Repatriates	C—Tax haven
D—United States	D—Masculinity	D—European Union (EU)	D—Inpatriates	D—Turnkey project
E—Japan	E—Long-term orientation	E—International Monetary Fund	E—International assignee	E—Balance of payments accounts
F—Canada	F—Hofstede	F—International Labor Organization (ILO)	F—President	F—Free trade
G—Mexico	G—Assertiveness	G—World Bank	G—Secretary of State	G—Exchange rate
H—England	H—Culture	H—International Accounting Standards Committee	H—An unwelcome person	H—Import quota
I—China	I—United States	I—World Court	I—Law among peoples	I—North American Free Trade Agreement (NAFTA)
J—South Korea	J—Scandinavia	J—Multinational corporation	J—law of the soil (nationality determined by birthplace)	J—Central American Free Trade Agreement (CAFTA)

Definition Matrix Game 3—Computers

Human Resource Information Systems (HRIS)	*HR Terms Seen in an HRIS*	*Computer Basics*	*Internet Behavior*	*Internet Features*
A—System used by human resources departments to track employees and information about them	A—When an employee works less than 100% of the time before he or she retires	A—Smallest piece of information used by the computer.	A—Online harassment	A—System designed to prevent unauthorized access to a private network
B—Software application that combines many human resources functions into one package.	B—When an employee is moved up to a higher position	B—System malfunction in which the computer stops working and has to be restarted.	B—Combination of hardware and software tools used for surveillance in the workplace	B—Identifier for a computer or device on a network
C—Software that allows an organization to use a system of integrated apps to manage the business	C—To bring back a previous employee	C—Temporary holding area where data is stored while it is being used or changed	C—Act of hacking in a website or computer to communicate a politically or socially motivated message	C—Any software that disables an advertisement window that you would see while using a browser
D—Any app that supports a specific business process and targets select users	D—Payment for extra work performed by an appointed employee	D—Files on disk that contain instructions for a computer	D—Software designed specifically to damage or disrupt a system, such as a virus	D—Network based on an internet belonging to an org. usually a corporation, accessible only to its members
E—Aggregation of the data from disparate sources	E—Academically secure status given to academics only	E—Large capacity storage device made of multiple disks housed in a rigid case	E—Exaggerated, omnipresent 24/7 electronic surveillance.	E—Business conducted over the Internet

Definition Matrix Game 3—Computers

Human Resource Information Systems (HRIS)	*HR Terms Seen in an HRIS*	*Computer Basics*	*Internet Behavior*	*Internet Features*
F—Computer-based system that provides managers with the tools to efficiently manage org. departments	F—Similar tasks that may apply to several different positions	F—System error that causes the cursor to lock in place	F—Company web document that details the personally identifiable information the company collects about its site visitors	F—Program or group of programs designed for the user
G—In software, this is a section of the program	G—Beginning date of employment	G—Graphic symbol for an application, file or folder.	G— Employees who surf the net, write e-mail at work that are not related to their job	G—Error in software or hardware that causes programs to not work
H—Software application that enables the electronic handling of recruitment needs	H—Personnel procedures such as hiring, promotion, and firing	H—To transfer data from one computer to another	H—Turned on and connected	H—Public space on transmission lines
I—HRIS module that includes classifications, raises, bonuses, and pay rates for employees	I—Report that will show any errors in employee data	I—Error that causes a program to behave in an unexpected way	I—Message which is written to deliberately spread fear, uncertainty and doubt.	I—These people try to keep users on or chat room free of personal insults
J—Actual Windows-based software which controls the data in the Retail, Accounting and HR modules	J—Smallest organizational unit for which a complete self-contained set of accounts can be drawn up for external reporting	J—Copy of a file or disk you make for archiving purposes	J—Automated process of proactively identifying vulnerabilities of network computing systems	J—Top social network in the world

Answer Matrix Game 3—Computers

Human Resource Information Systems (HRIS)	*HR Terms Seen in an HRIS*	*Computer Basics*	*Internet Behavior*	*Internet Features*
A—Human resource information systems (HRIS)	A—Phased retirement	A—Bit	A—Cyberbullying	A—Firewall
B—Human resource management systems (HRMS)	B—Promotion	B—Crash	B—Cyberveillance	B—IP address
C—Enterprise resource planning (ERP)	C—Rehire	C—Memory	C—Hacktivism	C—Pop-up blocker
D—Vertical application	D—Stipend	D—Software	D—Malware	D—Intranet
E—Data virtualization	E—Tenure	E—Hard drive	E—Ubberveillance	E—Ecommerce
F—Management Information System (MIS)	F—Jobs	F—Freeze	F—Privacy Statement	F—Application
G—Module	G—Original hire date	G—Icon	G—Cyberloafing	G—Bug
H—Applicant Tracking System (ATS)	H—Personnel actions	H—Download	H—Online	H—Cloud
I—Payroll	I—Data verification report	I—Bug	I—Hoax	I—Moderators
J—Systems Applications Products (SAP)	J—Company code	J—Backup	J—Vulnerability scanning	J—Facebook

Definition Matrix Game 4—Planning and Design

Financial Measurement	*Strategic Plans*	*Organizational Structures*	*Math Charts and Analyses*	*Workforce Planning*
A—Statement covering revenues minus expenses equals profits	A—Promise to be the lowest cost producer in the industry	A—Companies separated based on product, customer, or region	A—Chart showing check marks to keep track of events	A—Chart showing present performance and promotability of inside candidates
B—Analysis to figure when revenue matches program costs	B—Belief that best opportunities come outside typical markets	B—Companies organized by IT, HR, accounting, etc.	B—Chart showing variations from normal	B—Card for each position to show replacements and their qualifications
C—Provides general view of org's finance, customers, processes, and learning	C—Make service different from the competition so a premium price can be paid	C—Number of employees reporting to the boss	C—Chart showing factors that affect problems or intended outcomes	C—Records showing employee's education, skills and interests
D—Net benefits of an act divided by the cost of the act	D—Identify a segment of the market and make sure the company serves that market	D—Degree to which control is at the top of the organization	D—Chart showing relationships between variables using dots	D—Economic need for workers in the market
E—Sum of the present values of the individual cash flows of the same entity.	E—Always be at the head of the market	E—Structure in which all employees must follow rules with little discretion	E—Chart showing relationships between two variables using bars	E—Amount of workers available in the market

Definition Matrix Game 4—Planning and Design

Financial Measurement	*Strategic Plans*	*Organizational Structures*	*Math Charts and Analyses*	*Workforce Planning*
F—Study of an organization's HR strategies and policies	F—Maximize efficiency and cost effectiveness	F—Degree to which lower levels have decision making authority	F—Analyses examining the relationship between a dep. variable and set of independent variables	F—Monthly document published by the U. S. Dept. of Labor showing occupational projections
G—Irrelevant costs	G—A strategy that cannot be used in more than one situation	G—Structure combining divisional and functional traits	G—A variable whose values are recorded over a period of time	G—Predictions of employments needs based on variables
H—Net income divided by equity	H—Strategy at the level of HR, finance, and IT	H—Authority line within an org.	H—Method of making decisions using data from a scientific study	H—Process of deciding how to fill jobs
I—Assets on left, liabilities and equity on right	I—Strategy dealing with the overall firm	I—Extent to which processes are divided into separate tasks and jobs	I—Analyses used to create selected number of unobserved variables	I—Quarterly published by the U. S. Dept. of Labor showing occupational projections
J—Profit remaining after all expenses have been subtracted	J—Strategy focusing on competitive positioning to create an advantage over competitors	J—Organization centered around a temporary endeavor	J—Procedure to test hypotheses about the relative proportion of cases falling into mutually exclusive groups	J—Relationships between the number of applicants, visits, interviewed, offers, and new hires

Answer Matrix Game 4—Planning and Design

Financial Measurement	*Strategic Plans*	*Organizational Structures*	*Math Charts and Analyses*	*Workforce Planning*
A—Income statement	A—Cost leadership	A—Divisional	A—Check sheet	A—Management replacement chart
B—Break-even analysis	B—Blue ocean	B—Functional	B—Control chart	B—Position replacement card
C—Balanced scorecard	C—Differentiation	C—Span of control	C—Cause and affect diagram	C—Skills inventories
D—Return on Investment (ROI)	D—Focus	D—Centralization	D—Scatter diagram	D—Labor demand
E—Net present value (NPV)	E—Product leadership	E—Formalization	E—Bar chart	E—Labor supply
F—HR Audit	F—Operational excellence	F—Decentralization	F—Regression	F—Monthly Labor Review
G—Sunk costs	G—Single use plan	G—Matrix	G—Time series variable	G—Labor forecasts
H—Return on equity	H—Functional	H—Chain of command	H—Hypothesis test	H—Workforce planning
I—Balance sheet	I—Corporate	I—Specialization	I—Factor Analysis	I—Occupational Outlook Quarterly
J—Net income	J—Business	J—Project management	J—Chi-Square	J—Yield pyramid

Definition Matrix Game 5—Job Analysis, Job Descriptions, and Careers

Job Analysis	*Job Descriptions*	*Types of Job Arrangements*	*Methods to Rearrange Jobs*	*Career Management*
A—Record of daily events to obtain information about a job	A—Dept. of Labor's website containing detailed job descriptions	A—Employees hired to work on a short-time basis	A—Moving to a higher level job	A—Senior colleague who provides informal advice to a junior colleague
B—Set of written questions to obtain information about job content	B—Performs other tasks as required	B—Employees hired to perform seasonal work on a short-time basis	B—Adding more tasks from different levels	B—Programs to help future leaders move quickly up the ladder
C—Meeting with an employee to obtain information about his/her job	C—One sentence summary of what the job does	C—Very skilled workers hired for long-term projects	C—Moving to a lower level job	C—Managing how people leave the organization
D—Act of seeing a person's work to obtain information about the job	D—Describes a job in a few words	D—Programs in which temps could become regular employees	D—Laterally moving to a new geographic location	D—Technical skills training often done through unions
E—Act of analyzing a person's work outputs to obtain information about the job	E—According to the ADA, tasks that must be in the job	E—Program in which two workers account for one full-time position	E—Cutting many jobs due to economic conditions	E—More formal one-on-one career assessment and counseling

Definition Matrix Game 5—Job Analysis, Job Descriptions, and Careers

Job Analysis	*Job Descriptions*	*Types of Job Arrangements*	*Methods to Rearrange Jobs*	*Career Management*
F—Shows the organization-wide work division	F—Statement of employee characteristics and qualifications needed for satisfactory performance	F—All employees get "laid off" part of the day to reduce expenses	F—Engineering track and managerial track, for example	F—Process in which a terminated worker gets guidance on how to get a new job
G—Provides a detailed picture of the work flow	G—KSAs stand for this	G—Employees who work less than the regular work week	G—Working conditions are so bad that the employee resigns	G—Final interview an employee receives when leaving the organization
H—Uses of job analysis in HR	H—Predecessor to O*NET	H—Employees who report to work only when called	H—Employer discharges an employee for whistleblowing or other lawful activities	H—Ability to keep talented employees in an organization
I—Systematic study of what tasks and conditions occur in each job	I—Used by Federal statistical agencies to classify workers into 840 occupational categories	I—Short-term employees who rotate various positions	I—Adding more tasks at the same skill level for a job	I—Process of initiating and sustaining employee career paths
J—Stands for PAQ	J—Prime source of internal information to help write job descriptions	J—Any person who performs services for the company when the company can control what will be done and how it will be done	J—Moving a person to different jobs at the same level	J—Last step in a person's career

Answer Matrix Game 5—Job Analysis, Job Descriptions, and Careers

Job Analysis	*Job Descriptions*	*Types of Job Arrangements*	*Methods to Rearrange Jobs*	*Career Management*
A—Diary	A—O*Net	A—Temporaries	A—Promotions	A—Mentor
B—Questionnaire	B—Elastic clause	B—Seasonal workers	B—Job enrichment	B—Fast track programs
C—Interview	C—Responsibility	C—Contractors	C—Demotions	C—Offboarding
D—Observation	D—Job title	D—Temp-to-hire programs	D—Transfers	D—Apprenticeship
E—Work sample	E—Essential job functions	E—Job sharing	E—Downsizing	E—Coaching
F—Organization chart	F—Job specification	F—Work sharing	F—Dual career ladders	F—Outplacement
G—Process chart	G—Knowledge, skills and abilities	G—Part-timers	G—Constructive discharge	G—Exit interview
H—Everything in HR	H—Dictionary of Occupational Titles	H—On-call employees	H—Retaliatory discharge	H—Retention
I—Job analysis	I—Standard Occupational Classification	I—Floaters	I—Job enlargement	I—Career management
J—Position Analysis Questionnaire	J—Job analysis	J—Employee	J—Job rotation	J—Late career

Definition Matrix Game 6—Equal Employment Opportunity

Complaint Process	*Americans With Disabilities Act*	*Laws*	*Immigration*	*Gender Discrimination*
A—Intentional discrimination	A—Person who is regarded as having an impairment	A—Prohibits discrimination based on genetic information	A—Most common document that establishes identity and employment authorization	A—Barriers keeping women from getting executive jobs
B—Individuals covered in federal or state antidiscrimination laws	B—Number of employees private sector companies need to have ADA apply	B—Prohibits discrimination based on pregnancy or childbirth	B—Internet-based system that allows employers to check employment eligibility	B—Principle that employers are legally responsible for discriminatory acts of their employees
C—Individual who has prima facie burden in a discrimination case	C—Modifying the job process to allow a disabled worker to do the job	C—Protects people how have had cancer from hiring discrimination	C—Law that establishes citizenship and employment authorization rules	C—Unwanted trading of sex for a pay increase
D—Unintentional discrimination	D—Task that is required within a job	D—Mentions that gamblers are not protected from discrimination	D—Common form U. S. citizens must fill out within 3 days of hire for work in the U. S.	D—Unwanted sexually explicit posters
E—Federal agency in charge of handling antidiscrimination laws	E—Amendment to ADA expanding the definition of disability	E—Give plaintiffs rights to a jury trial	E—Temporary visa for nonimmigrant workers to hire highly skilled workers	E—Chemicals that can cause damage to the fetus

Definition Matrix Game 6—Equal Employment Opportunity

Complaint Process Terms	*Americans With Disabilities Act*	*Laws*	*Immigration*	*Gender Discrimination*
F—Entity accused of discrimination in a case	F—If reasonable accommodation cannot be done, then this occurs	F—Creates a updated time frame for filing wage discrimination claims	F—Immigrant visas for aliens with extraordinary ability	F—Only male actors are hired due to this rule
G—Under Title VII, a claim must be file within these number of days	G—Agency enforcing ADA	G—Requires discrimination laws to apply to employees of Congress	G—Visas reserved for students	G—Pregnancy is not a handicap according to this law
H—Agency that monitors federal contractors to see if they follow affirmative action guidelines	H—Earlier public sector related disability discrimination act	H—Prohibits discrimination against individuals 40 or over	H—For immigration, this is evidence that a driver's license establishes	H—Another name for the 4/5ths rule
I— Damages exceeding simple compensation and awarded to punish the defendant	I—Women's condition protected in a 1978 act not considered a disability	I—Prohibits discrimination based on race, color, religion, gender, or national origin	I—For immigration, this is evidence that a U. S. Social Security Card establishes	I—Agency that deals with sexual discrimination complaints for those working in the private sector
J—Practice of legally not hiring a person due to religion, gender, or national origin of a person	J—Examples of this include mobility, bathing, and caring for oneself	J—Protects individuals who have worked in the armed services in terms of employment	J—Authorization applied to a passport, permitting entry into a particular country	J—Court case that stated sexual harassment violates Title VII of the Civil Rights Act of 1964

Answer Matrix Game 6—Equal Employment Opportunity

Complaint Process Terms	*Americans With Disabilities Act*	*Laws*	*Immigration*	*Gender Discrimination*
A—Disparate treatment	A—Disabled person	A—Genetic Information Nondiscrimination Act	A—Passport	A—Glass ceiling
B—Protected class	B—15	B—Pregnancy Discrimination Act	B—E-verify	B—Vicarious liability
C—Plaintiff	C—Reasonable accommodation	C—Americans with Disabilities Act	C—Immigration Reform and Control Act	C—Quid pro quo sexual harassment
D—Adverse impact	D—Essential job function	D—Americans With Disabilities Act	D—I-9	D—Hostile environment sexual harassment
E—Equal Employment Opportunity Commission	E—ADAAA	E—Civil Rights Act of 1991	E—H-1B	E—Teratogens
F—Defendant	F—Undue hardship	F—Lilly Ledbetter Fair Pay Act	F—EB-1	F—Business necessity
G—180 days	G—EEOC	G—Congressional Accountability Act	G—F-1	G—Americans With Disabilities Act
H—Office of Federal Contract Compliance Programs	H—Vocational Disability Act	H—Age Discrimination in Employment Act	H—Identity	H—80% rule
I—Punitive damages	I—Pregnancy	I—Civil Rights Act of 1964	I—Employment authorization	I—EEOC
J—Bona fide occupational qualification	J—Major life activities	J—Uniformed Services Employment and Reemployment Rights Act	J—Visa	J—Meritor Savings Bank vs. Vinson

Definition Matrix Game 7—Recruiting

Recruiting Methods I	*Recruiting Methods II*	*Alternative Staffing Methods*	*Analysis*	*Miscel-laneous*
A—Job candidates who apply by walking inside companies	A—Internal recruiting method allowing employees to show an interest in a job before it is available	A—Those who work less than full-time	A—Ratio showing success at each step in the recruiting process	A—Process of finding new employees
B—These organizations are noted for their hiring halls and apprenticeship programs	B—Having current employees recommend others for any job openings	B—Those who offer companies services but pay full Social Security	B—The total amount companies have to pay per person to hire them	B—Creating a distinctive image for the company
C—Free employee/employer referral services through state Department of Labors	C—Inexpensive daily "fishwrap" often used to advertise local jobs	C—Moving the HR function to another company that specializes in HR	C—Summary of the responsibilities, tasks, and specifications of a job	C—Collection of data on employees that can be searched and retrieved via computer
D—Recruiting via placing a sign in front of the company doorway in front of customers/clients	D—Placing openings on a bulletin board for existing employees	D—Example of this type of work is garden that occurs only during warm weather	D—Exercise within an assessment center that features memos that participants have to prioritize	D—Interviews that collect data about employees as they leave the company
E—Source of recruits who are pursuing degrees	E—Computerized inventory of employee qualifications	E—Using a staffing agency to help hire regular employees	E—Number of people hired to replace people who leave	E—Recruiting outside of the company

Definition Matrix Game 7 Continued—Recruiting

Recruiting Methods I	*Recruiting Methods II*	*Alternative Staffing Methods*	*Analysis*	*Miscel-laneous*
F—Using Forbes, Fortune as a recruiting method	F—Most popular Internet recruiting website	F— Using the services of a vendor to provide all or some of their employees for a fee	F—Department of Labor website showing job descriptions and providing citizens with a skills search	F—Examples include bidding, posting, skill banks, promotions and referrals
G—Involves commercials and incorporates sight and sound	G—Monster is an example of this recruiting method	G— Practice of working at home and linking to the org. via computer	G—Access over a million jobs with this federal government Internet site	G—Movement of an employee from one level of the company to a higher level
H—College conferences in which many employers get together to recruit	H—Companies that help laid off employees get jobs	H—Employees who go to work only when the company requests their services	H—Principal fact-finding agency for the Federal Government in labor economics and statistics	H—Leading provider of online recruiting services for technology, engineering
I—Firms specializing in executive recruitment	I—Companies that place employees who work for short designated periods in companies	I—Staffing methods that go beyond regular full-time employees	I—Recruitment technique in which employees receive a finder's fee for finding an employee	I—Network of local, state, and national service programs
J—Weekly recruiting tabloid published through the Wall Street Journal	J—Programs that allow companies to partner with schools to provide a quality labor pool	J—Employment arrangement in which responsibility and liability over employees is shared between the employer and a staffing agency	J—Center that determines who might be eligible for promotions. Management-related exercises such as the in-basket are used	J—Pool of qualified retired employees who are occasionally able to be rehired

Answer Matrix Game 7—Recruiting

Recruiting Methods I	*Recruiting Methods II*	*Alternative Staffing Methods*	*Analysis*	*Miscel-laneous*
A—Walk-ins	A—Bidding	A—Part-time employees	A—Yield ratio	A—Recruiting
B—Labor unions/union hiring halls	B—Referrals	B—Independent contractors	B—Cost per hire	B—Branding
C—Job Service/state agencies	C—Newspapers	C—Outsourcing	C—Job description	C—Database
D—Point of purchase/contact	D—Job posting	D—Seasonal work	D—In-basket exercise	D—Exit interviews
E—Colleges/universities	E—Skill banks	E—Payrolling	E—Turnover	E—External recruiting
F—Magazines	F—Monster.com	F—Employee leasing	F—O*NET	F—Internal recruiting
G—Television and radio	G—Internet	G—Telecommuting	G—CareerOneStop or CareerInfoNet	G—Promotion
H—College fairs, university fairs, or job fairs	H—Outplacement firms	H—On-call workers	H—Bureau of Labor Statistics	H—Dice.com
I—Headhunters or executive search firms	I—Temporary agencies	I—Alternative or flexible staffing methods	I—Bounty program	I—AmeriCorps
J—National Business Employment Weekly	J—School to work programs	J—Co-employment or joint employment	J—Assessment center	J—Retiree skill bank

Definition Matrix Game 8—Selection

Selection Laws	*Documents*	*Numbers*	*Discrimination*	*Organizations*
A—Act associated with teratogens	A—Annual summary of workplace accidents and illnesses	A—Law title focusing on discrimination in the workplace	A—Unwanted sexual requests or hostile environment	A—EEOC is under this department
B—Act associated with gender, race, religion, color, and national origin	B—Government guidelines for employment testing	B—Detailed report of specific workplace accidents and illnesses	B—Principle supporting male-only bathroom attendant jobs	B—Enforcement agency for the Equal Pay Act
C—Act associated with the general duty to keep a safe work environment	C—Required equal employment report for companies with 100 or more employees	C—Executive order prohibiting federal contractors from discriminating based on race, color, etc.	C—Doing extra, without undue hardship, to assist handicapped individuals to do their job	C—Agency responsible for enforcing executive orders
D—Act banning quotas and defining punitive damages	D—Short term plan for how an organization will meet its goals	D—Granted all persons the same property rights as white citizens	D—Strict formulas assigned to hire minorities	D—Agency responsible for inspecting employers and applying safety standards
E—Under this law, employers must reemploy workers who left jobs to fulfill military duties	E—Report summarizing how to handle and dispose of chemicals	E—Amendment forbidding states from taking life, liberty, and property without due process	E—Hypothesis testing to see if appropriate hiring was done based on relevant population figures	E—Government research institute on safety and health

Definition Matrix Game 8 Continued—Selection

Selection Laws	*Documents*	*Numbers*	*Discrimination*	*Organizations*
F—Law associated with "40 and above"	F—Form where you write details about an accident or injury	F—Ratio rule that helps determine adverse impact	F—Giving minorities additional points on selection tests—made illegal by a 1990's act	F—Organization that rules on union representation elections
G—Law protecting veterans who fought in Vietnam	G—Passport will satisfy evidence required for this immigration form	G—Another name for the four-fifths rule	G—Person who applies for a job	G—Executive branch department where the Bureau of Labor Statistics is housed
H—Private sector handicapped law	H—Log of injuries or illnesses form	H—The Civil Rights Act of 1964 requires this many employees	H—Barrier women have in getting to higher level jobs	H—Final court that ruled on Griggs vs. Duke Power
I—Public sector handicapped law	I—Basic form that employees complete to apply for jobs	I—Age Discrimination Act requires this many employees	I—Gender, color, national origin, race, and something else	I—Second highest court in the United States
J—Associated with lie detector tests	J—A job applicant-created summary of work history and background	J—FMLA requires this many employees	J—ADA and the Vocational Rehabilitation Act have this protected group in common	J—Organization with home base that maintains centers in different countries to reduce costs

Answer Matrix Game 8—Selection

Selection Laws	*Documents*	*Numbers*	*Discrimination*	*Organizations*
A—Pregnancy Discrimination Act	A—OSHA Form 300A	A—Title VII	A—Sexual harassment	A—Department of Justice
B—Civil Rights Act of 1964	B—Uniform Guidelines	B—OSHA Form 301	B—BFOQ	B—EEOC
C—Occupational Safety and Health Act	C—EEO-1 report	C—Executive Order 11246	C—Reasonable accommodation	C—OFCCP
D—Civil Rights Act of 1991	D—Action steps	D—Civil Rights Act of 1866	D—Quotas	D—OSHA
E—Uniformed Services Employment and Reemployment Rights Act	E—Material Safety Data Sheets	E—Fourteenth Amendment	E—Utilization analysis	E—NIOSH
F—Age Discrimination Act	F—OSHA form 301	F—80 percent rule	F—Race norming	F—NLRB
G—Vietnam Veterans Readjustment Act	G—I-9 form	G—EEO-1 report	G—Applicant	G—Department of Labor
H—Americans With Disabilities Act	H—OSHA 300 form	H—15 or more employees	H—Glass ceiling	H—Supreme Court
I—Vocational Rehabilitation Act	I—Application form	I—20 or more employees	I—Religion	I—Court of Appeals
J—Polygraph Protection Act	J—Resume	J—50 or more employees	J—Handicap	J—Multinational corporation

Definition Matrix Game 9—Training and Development

Developing the Organization	*Adult Learning*	*Motivation*	*Assessment of Needs*	*Program Design and Development*
A—Providing job specific knowledge and skills	A—Years of this is associated with working in companies	A—According to Maslow, this is the need for respect	A—Identifies knowledge, skills, and abilities needed in an organization's future	A—Clear statement starting with the letter G of the purpose of the program
B—Legal right of an author to keep others from copying his or her work	B—Readiness to learn	B—A Belief that if you work hard you will do well	B—Second step in The ADDIE model	B—Type of training in which students act out a concept
C—First step in starting a business	C—Those who learn best through seeing	C—According to Maslow, the need to feel protected from threats	C—Identifies knowledge, skills, and abilities and individual needs to have a future in the organization	C—Most common type of training in which new employees are introduced to the organization
D—What an organization intents to become more than five years from now	D—Act of breaking information down to understand it	D—Belief that if you do well you will be rewarded	D—Step in ADDIE model when materials are created	D—Type of training in unions to learn a trade by combining work experience with some classroom
E—Examples of these include honesty, integrity, hard work, timeliness	E—Those who learn best through hearing	E—Continued absence of a response to an action	E—Instrument allowing companies to collect training needs data based on responses from employees	E—Type of training in which an instructor shows all of the correct steps in completing a task

Definition Matrix Game 9—Training and Development

Developing the Organization	*Adult Learning*	*Motivation*	*Assessment of Needs*	*Program Design and Development*
F—Deeply ingrained assumptions that influence our actions	F—According to the Age Discrimination Act, these individuals should not be discriminated against in training programs	F—Strength of one's desire for a particular outcome	F—ADDIE step in which the program is delivered to the target audience	F—Type of training in which a company goes to a class to have students work on a company
G—Conceptual type of thinking that helps one see how to change patterns	G—Level of learning where one is able to respond to new situations	G—This occurs when a person works to avoid an undesirable outcome	G—Identifies how well An employee competed his or her tasks	G—Type of training in which students read about a realistic situation and then analyze It
H—Individuals who develop new companies	H—Highest level in Maslow's Need Hierarchy	H—Theory in which a person compares his or her pay with others	H—The final step in the ADDIE Model	H—Ability to learn or acquire a skill
I—Legal right of inventors to keep others from benefiting from their work	I—Theory of adult learning	I—Theory based on studies about characteristics of high achievers	I—Identifies needs that will help the organization accomplish its objectives	I—Type of training that can be completely unstructured but can help with personal skills
J—Process of enhancing the effectiveness of an organization	J—Those who learn best through hands-on interaction	J—Theory About the ability to execute a necessary course of action	J—Assessment method beginning with the letter F that allows interaction between viewpoints	J—Training that widens the circle of inclusion to tap the wealth of a broad talent base

Answer Matrix Game 9—Training and Development

Developing the Organization	*Adult Learning*	*Motivation*	*Assessment of Needs*	*Program Design and Development*
A—Training	A—Experience	A—Esteem	A—Organizational assessment	A—Goal
B—Copyrights	B—Trainability	B—Expectancy	B—Design	B—Role play
C—Mission	C—Visual learners	C—Safety/security	C—Individual assessment	C—Orientation
D—Vision	D—Analysis	D—Instrumentality	D—Development	D—Apprenticeships
E—Values	E—Auditory learners	E—Extinction	E—Survey	E—Demonstration
F—Mental models	F—40 and above	F—Valence	F—Implementation	F—Live or living case
G—Systems thinking	G—Synthesis	G—Negative reinforcement	G—Performance appraisals	G—Case study
H—Entrepreneurs	H—Self-actualization	H—Equity theory	H—Evaluation	H—Aptitude
I—Patents	I—Andragogy theory	I—McClelland's theory	I—Needs analysis	I—T-groups, training groups or sensitivity training
J—Organizational development	J—Kinesthetic learners	J—Self-efficacy theory	J—Focus groups	J—Diversity training

Definition Matrix Game 10—Performance Appraisal

Methods	*Errors*	*Quality Tools*	*Testing*	*Miscellaneous*
A—Most common category rating method	A—Rating a person high because of one characteristic he/she has	A—Strategic system for integrating quality and customer satisfaction in companies	A—Written questions to obtain information about an employee	A—Performance tests based on looking at the outputs from work such as reports, diagrams, and products
B—Test question requiring an answer in the form of a sentence, paragraph, or longer composition	B—Rating a person low because of one characteristic he/she has	B—European-based quality standards	B—Group used for testing proposes that receives no training	B—Summary of the activities of an employee at certain times of the day
C—Rating scale anchored by desirable and undesirable behaviors	C—Rating everyone roughly average when a wider range is more accurate	C—To achieve this, production must be less than 3.4 defects per million	C—Feedback in which everyone an employee influences can appraise that person	C—Placing employees in order of performance
D—Analysis of an employee's productivity based on some standard	D—Rating everyone low when a higher range is more accurate	D—Visual representation of the factors thought to influence problems	D—Group used for testing purposes that receives unrelated training	D—American-based awards for quality
E—List of desirable and undesirable incidents associated with an employee over time for appraisal purposes	E—Rating a person only based on initial contact with that person	E—Graphical representation of variations from normal over time	E—Least difficult though least useful data to collect about program performance	E—Process of improving organizational effectiveness through planned changes

Definition Matrix Game 10 Continued—Performance Appraisal

Methods	*Errors*	*Quality Tools*	*Testing*	*Miscellaneous*
F—HR interviews supervisors of each employee and then tabulates comparison ratings	F—Rating everyone high when a lower range is more accurate	F—Frequency distribution represented by a series of rectangles	F—Testing before training begins	F—Examination
G—Comparing two people at a time to develop a ranking	G—Rating a person based on the latest visit with that person	G—Two-dimensional graph consisting of points associated with x and y values	G—Response of an employee to his or her environment	G—Act of watching employee behavior
H—Placing specific percentages of people in to categories such as high, medium, and low	H—Rating a person relative to others rather than standard objectives	H—Graphical representation of two variables using rectangles	H—According to Kirkpatrick, this is the most difficult though most useful data to collect about program performance	H—Mock-up of a system in order to examine the functioning of a real system
I—Appraiser checks off activities or characteristics of the employee through this method	I—Rating a person low based on his/her protected status	I—Graphical representation of how items contribute to the total effect	I—Knowledge or skill gained from instruction	I—Circumstances not in the employee's control that affect the employee's performance
J—Employees and managers mutually agree on employee objectives to be evaluated after performance	J—Rating a person high due to similarity with the rater	J—Graphical representation of trends over a time period	J—Testing after training is completed; often compared to a pretest	J—Statistical analysis of changes over time. May include factors such as seasonality

Answer Matrix Game 10—Performance Appraisal

Methods	*Errors*	*Quality Tools*	*Testing*	*Miscellaneous*
A—Graphic rating scale	A—Halo	A—Total quality management	A—Questionnaire	A—Work sample tests
B—Essay	B—Horn	B—ISO 9000	B—Control group	B—Diary (log)
C—Behaviorally anchored rating scales (BARS)	C—Central tendency	C—Six Sigma	C—360 degree feedback	C—Ranking
D—Performance appraisal	D—Strictness	D—Cause and effect diagram	D—Placebo group	D—Malcolm Baldrige Awards
E—Critical incidents	E—First impression	E—Control chart	E—Reaction	E—Organizational development
F—Field review	F—Leniency	F—Histogram	F—Pretest	F—Test
G—Paired comparison	G—Recency	G—Scatter diagram	G—Behavior	G—Observation
H—Forced distribution	H—Contrast (order)	H—Bar graph	H—Results	H—Simulation
I—Checklist	I—Discrimination (bias)	I—Pareto chart	I—Learning	I—Context
J—Management by objectives (MBO)	J—Same-as-me (similar-to-me)	J—Run chart	J—Posttest	J—Time series analysis

Definition Matrix Game 11—Compensation I

Pay	*Incentives*	*Begins with "C"*	*Compensation Laws*	*Measuring Tools*
A—Hiring affordability	A—Pay for performance for a group of individuals working together for a common goal	A—HR function that deals with every type of reward employees receive for doing organizational tasks	A—Act stating that equal jobs should be paid equally	A—Organized summary of tasks and specifications of a job
B—Restricted pay information within an organization	B—Organization-wide incentive program based on some measure of productivity	B—Job characteristics that organizations are willing to pay for such as effort	B— Act setting minimum wage and overtime standards	B—Standards that give employees targets to shoot for
C—Graph showing pay grade locations	C—Organization-wide incentive program in which employees receive shares of stock	C—Narrowing of the ratios of pay between jobs	C—Involves federal contractors supplying goods exceeding $10,000 annually	C—Organized way to check the relative worth of jobs
D—Analysis of market rates through an instrument	D—A system for providing both financial and non-financial rewards to employees	D—Limiting expenses	D—Involves federal contractors involved in construction with a contract value over $2000	D—Study conducted to determine how fast a job should be done
E—Pay increases based on performance appraisal ratings	E—Organization-wide incentive program in which employees receive a bonus based on a percentage of profits	E—Pay system in which workers are paid based on their skills and knowledge	E—Involves federal contractors providing services with a contract value over $2500	E—Method of studying how a job is done

Definition Matrix Game 11—Compensation I

Pay	*Incentives*	*Begins with "C"*	*Compensation Laws*	*Measuring Tools*
F—Method of paying for services or products online—used by Ebay	F—Rewards a person receives outside the job itself such as compensation	F—Type of job evaluation method used by the federal government	F—1916 Act concerning employment of young people	F—As opposed to a median, this statistic is affected by outliers
G—The level of income an individual receives	G—Incentive plan based on working fewer than expected hours	G—Plan in which employees get choices	G—Protects five categories of discriminated groups	G—The middle number in a distribution
H—Its length involves pay and width involves points	H—Incentive plan based on relationship between labor costs and sales value of production	H—Payment based on achieving certain standards	H—Limits deductions to executives to 1 million dollars	H—Most frequent level in a distribution
I—Line anchoring the geographic center of pay grades	I—Incentive plan where employees assume some of the risk of bad years	I—Plan where both the employee and employer contribute to the employee's pension	I—Protects employees 40 and over for pay purposes	I—Square root of the variance
J—When new employees receive equal or more pay than established	J—Incentive plan based on team or group production	J—Competency based on what is central to the organization's needs and objectives	J—Provided tax incentives for IRAs	J—High plus low divided by two

Answer Matrix Game 11—Compensation I

Pay	*Incentives*	*Begins with "C"*	*Compensation Laws*	*Measuring Tools*
A—Ability to pay	A—Team incentives	A—Compensation	A—Equal Pay Act	A—Job descriptions
B—Pay secrecy	B—Gain sharing	B—Compensable factor	B—Fair Labor Standards Act	B—Workload standards
C—Pay structure	C—Employee stock ownership plans	C—Compression	C—Walsh-Healy Act	C—Job evaluation
D—Pay survey	D—Organizational reward systems	D—Cost containment	D—Davis Bacon Act	D—Time study
E—Merit pay	E—Profit sharing	E—Competency based pay	E—MacNamara-O'Hara Service Contract Act	E—Motion study
F—Pay Pal	F—Extrinsic rewards	F—Classification method	F—Child Labor Act	F—Average, mean
G—Pay level	G—Improshare	G—Cafeteria-style plan	G—Civil Rights Act of 1964	G—Median
H—Pay grade	H—Scanlon plan	H—Commission	H—Revenue Reconciliation Act of 1993	H—Mode
I—Pay policy line	I—Risk sharing	I—Contributory plan	I—Age Discrimination in Employment Act	I—Standard deviation
J—Pay compression	J—Team (group) incentives	J—Core competency	J—Revenue Act of 1978	J—Midrange

Definition Matrix Game 12—Compensation II

Executive Pay	*Job Analysis*	*Pay Structures*	*Job Evaluation*	*International Compensation*
A— One time pay boost for performance	A—Effort to find out the requirements of a job	A—High pay minus low pay within a pay grade	A—Placing jobs in order of difficulty	A—Expatriate premium for working in another country
B—Hypothetical company stock	B—Competence to do a physical act	B—Pay above the pay grade as an exception	B—Job characteristic-oriented criteria by which jobs are compared in point systems	B—Expatriate premium for working in a country with difficult conditions
C—Special benefits for executives such as the company car	C—Department of Labor's online database of job descriptions replacing the Dictionary of Occupational Titles	C—Occurs when pay spread between experienced and inexperienced employees is small	C—Quantitative job evaluation system associated adding up the scores of each compensable factor	C—Approach to allow expatriates a similar standard of living in another country
D—Serves shareholders by analyzing top executive decisions	D—O*NET's model that summarizes how jobs will be described	D—Halfway point of each pay grade	D—Point system with know-how, problem-solving, and accountability as compensable factors	D—Pay adjustment for inflation
E—Government organization that collects taxes	E—Department of Labor's catalog of job descriptions that is being replaced by O*NET and the SOC	E—Within pay structures, these have a width and range	E—Category of job evaluation system used by the federal government	E—American workers sent to another country by an American company

Definition Matrix Game 12—Compensation II

Executive Pay	*Job Analysis*	*Pay Structures*	*Job Evaluation*	*International Compensation*
F—Theory that the winner or top manager should get much of the money	F—According to the Dictionary of Occupational Titles, these include data, people, and things	F—Pay structure associated with fewer, wider pay grades	F—Quantitative job evaluation system in which dollar values are assigned for each compensable factor for each job	F—German workers working in Germany for an American company
G—Example of this type of employee includes a five percent owner of the employer	G—Job analysis technique involving day-by-day listing of activities	G—Two sets of pay grades associated with two pay lines in a pay structure	G—Well-known jobs with established market pay used for comparisons with other jobs	G—Reestablishing an expatriate back to the home country
H—Incentives to help executives in case of a merger	H—194 question process-oriented questionnaire	H—Average of the pay grade divided by the midpoint	H—Purposely aligning job evaluation to match pay purposes such as market pay	H—Increase in the price of products in the economy
I—Stock plan requiring executives to not have ownership of company stock over a period	I—Describes 23 occupational groups	I—Regression line showing the relationship between market pay and points	I—Different point levels for each compensable factor	I—French workers working in Germany for an American Company
J—Incentives to keep executives in their job	J—Required job tasks according to the Americans with Disabilities Act	J—Range of pay in common between two pay grades	J—Specific name for the federal government's job classification system	J—Valuing one currency versus another

Answer Matrix Game 12—Compensation II

Executive Pay	*Job Analysis*	*Pay Structures*	*Job Evaluation*	*International Compensation*
A—Bonuses	A—Job analysis	A—Pay range	A—Ranking	A—Foreign service premium
B—Phantom stock	B—Skills	B—Red circle	B—Compensable factors	B—Hardship allowance
C—Perks	C—O*NET	C—Compression	C—Point method	C—Balance sheet approach
D—Board of directors	D—Content model	D—Midpoint	D—Hay System	D—Cost of living allowance
E—Internal Revenue Service	E—Dictionary of Occupational Titles	E—Pay grades	E—Job classification system	E—Expatriate
F—Tournament theory	F—Worker functions	F—Broadbanding	F—Factor comparison system	F—Host country or local national
G—Key employee	G—Diary	G—Two-tier pay	G—Benchmark or key jobs	G—Repatriation
H—Golden parachutes	H—Position Analysis Questionnaire	H—Compa-ratio	H—Policy capturing	H—Inflation
I—Restricted stock	I—Standard Occupational Classification	I—Market pay line	I—Factor degrees	I—Third country national
J—Golden handcuffs	J—Essential job functions	J—Overlap	J—General Schedule	J—Exchange rate

Definition Matrix Game 13—Benefits

Defined Contribution Plans	*Health Care I*	*Heath Care II*	*Benefits Laws*	*Miscellaneous*
A— Defined contribution plans for for-profit companies. These are tax exempt and authorized by section 401(K) of the IRS code	A—Managed care program with one center in which patients pay a co-payment.	A—Amount employees must pay for health expenses before health insurance begins to pay	A—Requires employers to provide alternative health coverage options associated with health maintenance organizations	A—Type of vesting in which employees go from zero percent to 100 percent vesting after a maximum of five years
B—Plan in which employees are given a share of the stock	B—Managed care program in which doctors provide services to a company at a discount.	B—Fixed amount of money employees must pay when they go to an HMO or PPO	B—Requires employers with 50 or more employees to give up to 12 weeks of unpaid leave for family medical issues	B—Type of vesting in which employees gradually go from zero percent to 100 percent after a maximum of seven years
C—Plan in which employers share the profits with employees	C—Plan that eliminates needless duplication of health benefits when spouses are under two health plans	C—Chinese medical treatment involved with inserting small needles in various parts of the body	C—Law introducing pension regulations and establishing vesting schedules and the PBGC	C—Mandatory insurance associated with workers who lose their job due to layoffs
D—Defined contribution plan when employers contribute a percentage regardless of profitability	D—Audit of hospital charges	D—Medical plans associated with orthodontia and teeth cleaning	D—Law allowing former employees to continue health care coverage through their prior company	D—According to the FMLA, a health condition that requires hospitalization
E—Retirement plans for individual wage-earners that are tax deferred	E—Medical conditions that occurred before signing up for health insurance	E—Health insurance coverage associated with long term medical disabilities	E—Law authorizing all employers to pay half of retirement benefits for employees	E—Period of time that employees get off for illnesses

Definition Matrix Game 13 Continued—Benefits

Defined Contribution Plans	*Health Care I*	*Heath Care II*	*Benefits Laws*	*Miscellaneous*
F—IRA accounts for self-employed and very small businesses	F—Program sponsored by employers to help employees with family, financial, or psychological counseling	F— Plan in which pretax dollars are applied to medical expenses usually not covered by health insurance	F— Amendment to the Age Discrimination in Employment Act that includes benefit protection	F—Pay employees receive for time off associated with Christmas, Fourth of July and related holidays
G—Defined contribution plans for charities defined by Section 403(b) of the IRS code.	G—Program sponsored by employers to help prevent illnesses through exercise and health monitoring	G—Health plans that provide employees choices	G—Law that tries to equalize mental and medical benefits	G—Type of pension plan covered by ERISA in which the employee will roughly know how much he/she will get upon retirement
H—Defined contribution plans for state employees determined by Section 457 of the IRS code	H—Health care focusing on the manipulation of the spine	H— Cafeteria plan— employee gets two or more completely different sets of choices	H—Law that requires a continuation of benefits for employees on active military duty	H—Medical care for the aged through the Social Security Administration
I—Retirement plans that qualify for tax exemption. Must provide employee benefits proportional to executives	I—Maximum money a health insurance company will pay for medical conditions	I— Maximum an employee would pay on his or her own in a given year	I—Law protecting the benefits rights of employees regardless of race, religion, national origin, gender, and color	I—Deferred benefit given only to highly compensated employees
J—Retirement plans in which you know how much you are contributing	J—Required benefit associated with on-the-job injuries or illnesses	J— Insurance-paid alternate analysis of the need for surgery	J—Law that changed ERISA pension vesting schedules and rollover rules	J—Private organization governing how financial information is to be reported

Answer Matrix Game 13—Benefits

Defined Contribution Plans	*Health Care I*	*Health Care II*	*Benefits Laws*	*Miscellaneous*
A—401(K)	A—HMO	A—Deductible	A—HMO Act	A—Cliff vesting
B—Employee Stock Ownership Plans	B—PPO	B—Co-payment	B—Family Medical Leave Act	B—Graded vesting
C—Profit sharing	C—Coordination of benefits	C—Acupuncture	C—Employee Retirement Income Security Act	C—Unemployment insurance
D—Money purchase	D—Utilization review	D—Dental plans	D—Consolidated Omnibus Budget Reconciliation Act	D—Serious health condition
E—Individual Retirement Accounts	E—Pre-existing conditions	E—Long-term disability coverage	E—Social Security Act	E—Sick leave
F—Simplified Employee Pensions	F—Employee assistance program	F—Flexible spending accounts	F—Older Workers' Benefit Protection Act	F—Holiday pay
G—403(b) plans	G—Wellness programs	G—Cafeteria plans	G—Mental Health Parity Act	G—Defined benefit plan
H—457 plans	H—Chiropractic care	H—Alternate dinners plan	H—Uniformed Services Employment and Reemployment Rights Act	H—Medicare
I—Qualified deferred compensation plans	I—Lifetime maximum benefit	I—Out-of-pocket maximum	I—Civil Rights Act of 1964	I—Nonqualified deferred compensation plan
J—Defined contribution plans	J—Workers' Compensation	J—Pre-certification or mandatory second opinion	J—Economic Growth and Tax Relief Reconciliation Act	J—Financial Accounting Standards Board

Definition Matrix Game 14—Employee Relations

Negotiation	*Discipline*	*Alternative Work Arrangements*	*Words Beginning with "P"*	*Good Employee Relations*
A—Third party neutral who makes binding decisions	A—Formal employee complaint against an employer	A—As a training technique, transferring a person from job to job at the same grade level	A—Management that openly asks for involvement from its employees	A—Employee guide that summarizes major policies
B—Third party neutral who makes no formal decisions	B—Type of discipline that starts with an oral warning, then written warning, suspension, and discharge	B—Allows employees to begin and end their workday as long as they complete certain hours	B—In a court case, the one who makes charges against the defendant	B—Policy in which employees can direct grievances to management
C—Third party neutral who makes nonbinding decisions	C—Discipline rule that includes a warning, consistent, impersonal, and immediate	C—Splitting a full-time job into two part-time jobs	C—Team that undertakes a specific plan or design	C—Laws ensuring public sector hearings are open to the public
D—Type of arbitration in which the arbitrator must choose one position or the other	D—Person who collects union grievances and dues within a union	D—Adding depth to a job	D—Bargaining that can occur among similar companies in the same industry	D—A device designed to get a large sample of employees to get them to share their opinions about company climate
E—Type of arbitration in which the arbitrator may choose a compromise position	E—Third party neutral who makes no rulings	E—Laying off everyone for a portion of each day	E—Arbitrator that stays with the company for cases on a continuing basis	E—In-depth, interactive interviews with about 8 to 12 people within an organization who discuss its products or services

Definition Matrix Game 14 Continued—Employee Relations

Negotiation	*Discipline*	*Alternative Work Arrangements*	*Words Beginning with "P"*	*Good Employee Relations*
F—One-case-only arbitrator	F—Last step in progressive discipline	F—Working 3/36 one week and 4/48 the next week is this	F—This review shifts human resource decisions from managers to peers of the grievant	F—Work teams that run their own operations
G—Involving multiple levels in negotiations in the public sector	G—Discipline associated with sending an employee to counseling programs to help fix a problem	G—Adding duties to the job that are of the same level	G—Subjects that management and unions do not have to negotiate	G—Container in which ideas for company improvement can be inserted
H—Public sector unions skipping management in negotiations and appealing to legislators	H—First step in progressive discipline	H—Working for a company while you are at home	H—Execution of an act	H—Physical board that shows announcements that can be tacked, stapled, or glued
I—Viewing the interests of both sides in negotiations as being in direct conflict	I—Detailed step-by-step processes	I—Regularly working less than a full-time job	I—Freedom from unacceptable intrusion	I—Process of developing job dimensions, relating jobs to other jobs, and documenting them in job descriptions
J—Bargaining tactic in which the union asks for more after each negotiation settlement	J—General statements outlined in employee handbooks	J—Reducing work hours and duties as retirement approaches	J—Repeated actions the employer has used over the years that is accepted by both union and management	J—Internal company display of jobs available

Answer Matrix Game 14—Employee Relations

Negotiation	*Discipline*	*Alternative Work Arrangements*	*Words Beginning with "P"*	*Good Employee Relations*
A—Arbitration	A—Grievance	A—Job rotation	A—Participative management	A—Employee handbook
B—Mediation	B—Progressive Discipline	B—Flextime	B—Plaintiff	B—Open door policy
C—Fact finding	C—Hot stove rule	C—Job sharing	C—Project team	C—Sunshine laws
D—Final offer arbitration	D—Union (or shop) steward	D—Job enrichment	D—Pattern bargaining	D—Employee (attitude or climate) surveys
E—Conventional Arbitration	E—Mediator	E—Work sharing	E—Permanent arbitrator	E—Focus groups
F—Ad hoc arbitrator	F—Discharge	F—Compressed work weeks	F—Peer review	F—Self-directed teams
G—Multilateral bargaining	G—Constructive discipline	G—Job enlargement	G—Permissive subjects	G—Suggestion boxes
H—End run bargaining	H—Oral warning	H—Telecommuting	H—Performance	H—Bulletin boards
I—Distributive (or zero sum, win lose) bargaining	I—Procedures	I—(Regular) part-time	I—Privacy	I—Job design
J—Whipsawing	J—Policies	J—Phased retirement	J—Past practice	J—Job posting

Definition Matrix Game 15—Labor Relations

Unfair Labor Practices	*Union Structures*	*Union Laws*	*Union-Management Rights*	*Union History*
A— Practice of creating jobs for no useful purpose	A—Found at the top of the AFL-CIO organizational chart	A—Law that supported elections for union officials	A—Illegal shop requiring union membership as a condition of employment	A—Court order requiring that a strike be stopped
B— Occurs when one company has subsidiaries that are unionized and non-unionized	B—Main union lobbying federation founded in 1955	B—Law that banned injunctions and yellow-dog contracts	B—Bans union shops in 22 states	B—Agreement that says you never joined a union and will never join a union
C—Doctrine used to determine how closely allied a secondary employer is to the primary employer	C—Permanent union employee who administers the contract and provides local union services	C—Law covering industrial relations in the airline industry	C—Contract clause for nonunion employees requiring a service fee to bargaining agents	C— First American court cases that did not declare unions to be an illegal constraint of trade
D—Strike occurring without official union approval	D—Person who typically collects union dues and organizes grievances	D—Law that helped establish right-to-work	D—Shop in which membership in the union must continue through the life of the contract	D—Set of three Supreme Court cases affirming the role of arbitration
E—Illegal strike in which many police officers call in sick when they are really not	E—Committee that hear employee grievances	E—1935 law that helped establish bargaining in the private sector	E—Contract clause requiring union membership after a certain period	E—Contract in which management gives the union leader money under the table in order to stop a strike

Definition Matrix Game 15 Continued—Labor Relations

Unfair Labor Practices	*Union Structures*	*Union Laws*	*Union-Management Rights*	*Union History*
F—An illegal but difficult to prove strike in which the employee reduces the speed of his or her work	F—Organization that consists of its members along with the president, steward, and business agent	F—Law covering industrial relations in the U. S. Postal Service	F—Statement in a contract in a right to work state that says that employees must join a union	F—U. S. President declares this if there is a strike that can drastically affect the United States
G—Strike in which pickets are in front of a building that contains several companies—one of which is involved in the strike	G—Non-union employees receiving certain benefits from the AFL-CIO	G—Law covering industrial relations in the Federal government	G—Union dues electronically deducted from members' pay	G—Steelworkers' Trilogy supported this
H—Illegal strike in which the employee stops working while in the place of work	H—The head of a local union	H—Law establishing minimum wage and overtime rules	H—Shop in which there are no union members	H—Union term associated with a strike breaker
I—Established guidelines for lawful picketing	I—A union with at least one branch outside of the United States	I—Law banning discrimination based on color	I—Subjects that must be bargained if the union requests it	I—Stoppage of work by union members
J—Goods produced by nonunion labor during a strike	J—Person who goes to the legislature to support a cause	J—Law banning attempts to overthrow the U. S. Government	J—Management preemptive tactic to close a plant before a union strike	J—Refusing to buy goods of a company in order to support some cause

Answer Matrix Game 15—Labor Relations

Unfair Labor Practices	*Union Structures*	*Union Laws*	*Union-Management Rights*	*Union History*
A—Featherbedding	A—National convention	A—Landrum-Griffin	A—Closed shop	A—Injunctions
B—Double breasting	B—AFL-CIO	B—Norris-LaGuardia	B—Right-to-work	B—Yellow dog contracts
C—Ally doctrine	C—Business agent	C—Railway Labor	C—Agency shop	C—Commonwealth vs. Hunt
D—Wildcat strike	D—Shop steward	D—Taft-Hartley	D—Maintenance of membership shop	D—Steelworkers' Trilogy
E—Blue flu	E—Grievance committee	E—Wagner	E—Union shop	E—Sweetheart contracts
F—Slowdown	F—Local	F—Postal Reorganization	F—Quasi-union shop	F—National emergency
G—Common situs picketing	G—Associate members	G—Civil Service Reform	G—Dues check off	G—Arbitration
H—Sit down strike	H—President	H—Fair Labor Standards	H—Open shop	H—Scab
I—Moore Dry Dock doctrine	I—International union	I—Civil Rights Act of 1964	I—Mandatory bargaining subjects	I—Strike
J—Hot cargo	J—Lobbyist	J—Smith	J—Lockout	J—Boycott

Definition Matrix Game 16—Health, Safety, Security

Health Hazards	*OSHA Terms*	*Security*	*Health Programs*	*Misc. Health, Safety, and Security*
A—Immune deficiency disease	A—OSHA form that is the log and summary of accidents and illnesses	A—Analysis of the chances of security violations	A—Program that provides mental counseling for employees	A—Physical or emotional exhaustion
B—"Common" illness associated with nasal passages not recordable under OSHA	B—Underground industry not covered by OSHA	B—1974 law protecting the privacy rights of employees	B—Policies to encourage employees to reduce nicotine intake	B—Act that requires pre-testing of certain new chemicals marketed each year
C—Internal reaction to perceived external pressures	C—Sheets associated with informing employees about the handling and disposing of chemicals in the workplace	C—Law focusing on electronic monitoring in the workplace	C—Good design of work equipment to reduce physical stress	C—Employer checking the location of each employee
D—Communicable disease caused by the tubercle bacillus that mostly affects the lungs	D—Top reason OSHA inspectors visit a company	D—Law on security stemming from the September 11 attacks creating a new department	D—Programs for employees that encourage good health before problems occur	D—Ages of individuals that are not allowed to work in physically dangerous jobs
E—A disease of the inflammation of the liver	E—Violation of safety where there is a great chance that death could occur	E—Alerting government agencies of illegal corporate activities	E—Health insurance programs that have a central location and provide for a co-payment	E—Unexpected occurrence causing injury

Definition Matrix Game 16 Continued—Health, Safety, Security

Health Hazards	*OSHA Terms*	*Security*	*Health Programs*	*Misc. Health, Safety, and Security*
F—Loss of feeling in the hands as a result of excessive computer mouse usage	F—Supreme Court case allowing employers to ask for warrants for OSHA inspections	F—Using a device to determine the truthfulness of statements	F—Wellness program that insure employees get shots to help with the flu	F—Violation of safety standards that would probably not cause death or serious injury
G—Disease associated with the lungs from work in the coal mines	G—Equipment that is used to protect one person	G—Physical acts against people	G—Training employees receive to help save other employees who have heart attacks	G—Complaints against the employer
H—Companies may discriminate against these workers who use nicotine	H—This organization recommends most of the standards adopted by OSHA	H—Agreement to keep certain information within the company	H—Health insurance programs that do not have a central location but where doctors provide employers health services at a discount with co-payments	H—Three digit phone number to contact help in case of emergency
I—Substances that can cause Cancer	I—OSHA clause to cover situations not addressed by specific standards	I—Primary individual who steals in companies	I—United States agency protecting the environment	I—OSHA form summarizing details of injuries or illnesses
J—Substances that can damage the fetus	J—Lowest level violation of safety standards	J—To protect facilities from unauthorized access	J—"Blue" company providing health care insurance	J—Positive, helpful stress

Answer Matrix Game 16—Health, Safety, and Security

Health Hazards	*OSHA Terms*	*Security*	*Health Programs*	*Misc. Health, Safety, and Security*
A—AIDS	A—Form 300	A—Vulnerability analysis	A—Employee assistance programs	A—Burnout
B— Common cold	B—Mining	B—Privacy Act of 1974	B—Smoking policies	B—Toxic Substance Control Act
C—Stress	C—MSDS	C—Electronic Communications Privacy Act	C—Ergonomics	C—Location monitoring
D—Tuberculosis	D—Imminent danger	D—Homeland Security Act	D—Wellness programs	D—Under 18 years old
E—Hepatitis	E—Serious violation	E—Whistle blowing	E—Health Maintenance Organizations	E—Accident
F—Carpal Tunnel Syndrome	F—Marshall vs. Barlows	F—Polygraph testing	F—Immunization programs	F—Other than serious violation
G—Black lung disease	G—Personal Protective Equipment	G—Violence	G—CPR	G—Grievances
H—Smokers	H—NIOSH	H—Confidentiality or nondisclosure agreement	H—Preferred Provider Organizations	H—911
I—Carcinogens	I—General Duty Clause	I—Employee theft	I—Environmental Protection Agency	I—Form 301
J—Taratogens	J—De minimis violation	J—Security	J—Blue Cross Blue Shield	J—Eustress

Definition Matrix Game 17—A Through E Words I

A	*B*	*C*	*D*	*E*
A—Statistical mean	A—Situation in which a company cannot meet its financial obligations	A—Sum of pay and benefits	A—Ways in which people differ across nationality, race or other factors	A—Agencies that help hire individuals
B—State of mind or disposition	B—Another name for a normal distribution curve	B—A benefit plan in which employees have many choices	B—Laying off people from work	B—Theory that consists of external, internal, and employee varieties
C—Leading union federation	C—Smallest piece of computer file data	C—In point systems, they include factors such as education and working conditions	C—Handicap	C—These individuals must pay half of Social Security but no unemployment insurance or worker's compensation
D—AA is associated with treatment of this problem	D—Type of disorder in which there are highs and lows	D—Act that initiated the Glass Ceiling Commission	D—Type of bargaining in which my win is your loss	D—Awareness of the ability to manage emotions and create motivation
E—Center to help select first level managers through a series of management simulations	E—Displacement of an employee through seniority rights	E—Minimum guaranteed pay employees receive when they come to work and there is no work	E—Sound level as defined by OSHA	E—Type of equity involved with seniority, incentives, and merit pay

Definition Matrix Game 17 Continued—A Through E Words I

A	*B*	*C*	*D*	*E*
F—Power to accomplish something	F—Obligation of a litigating party to establish facts	F—Sequenced series of jobs within a company to allow employees to move up	F—Employees who linger in their jobs by not doing much	F—Positive, helpful stress
G—Shop in which employees must pay a union a fee after joining the company after a certain period of time	G—Generation born sometime between 1946 and 1964	G—Unions focused on skilled employees	G—Money transferred to charity	G—Applied science of modifying equipment to improve productivity and reduce fatigue
H—Unexpected event resulting in harm	H—Actions or reactions of a person to stimuli	H—Artificial person, created by laws, that exists separate from its members	H—Along with exercise, a good version of this maintains good health	H—Act containing concepts such as portability and fiduciary responsibility
I—Overall result of employer practices that result in few minorities being hired	I—Tactic inspired by a General Electric manager when negotiators hear to but dismiss the other side's point of view	I—Type of validity in which you measure the predictor and criterion at the same time	I—Theory that says all behavior is motivated by drives such as sex, hunger, and thirst and based on rewards of past behavior	I—Theory that includes valence and instrumentality
J—Concentrating on the other person's message, feelings, and underlying communications	J—Comparing your company to the best practices of other companies	J—Union security measure requiring union membership at the time of hire	J—Career management approach in which there are two ways to move up in an org.	J—Law that bans pay differentials based on gender for identical jobs

Answer Matrix Game 17—A Through E Words

A	*B*	*C*	*D*	*E*
A—Average	A—Bankruptcy	A—Compensation	A—Diversity	A—Employment agencies
B—Attitude	B—Bell-shaped curve	B—Cafeteria plan	B—Downsizing	B—Equity theory
C—AFL-CIO	C—Bit	C—Compensable factors	C—Disability	C—Employees
D—Alcoholism	D—Bipolar disorder	D—Civil Rights Act of 1991	D—Distributive bargaining	D—Emotional Intelligence
E—Assessment center	E—Bumping	E—Call-in pay	E—Decibels	E—Employee equity
F—Ability	F—Burden of proof	F—Career ladders or paths	F—Deadwood	F—Eustress
G—Agency shop	G—Baby Boomer	G—Craft unions	G—Donations	G—Ergonomics
H—Accident	H—Behavior	H—Corporation	H—Diet	H—Employee Retirement Income Security Act
I—Adverse impact	I—Boulwarism	I—Concurrent validity	I—Drive theory	I—Expectancy theory
J—Active listening	J—Benchmarking	J—Closed shop	J—Dual career ladders	J—Equal Pay Act

Definition Matrix Game 18—A Through E Words II

A	*B*	*C*	*D*	*E*
A—Natural talent to do an activity	A—Grouping people together and treating them the same	A—Type of shop in which union membership Is required to be employed	A—Collection of computer information set up for rapid retrieval	A—In training evaluation, This evaluated group is compared with control and placebo groups
B—Arbitrators for one case only	B—Rating scale anchored by behaviors	B—Statistic that attempts to establish relationships between two variables	B—Redistributing an HR department from one location to many company branches	B—Example of this order includes 11246
C—Type of shop in which employees pay union dues but are not required to join	C—Workers involved in physical factory jobs	C—Two types of this validity include predictive and concurrent	C—Statistical analysis that arrives at a combination of variables that result in the largest separation of groups of individuals	C—Test in which each question leads to a narrative or short answer
D—Theory of adult learning	D—One-time increase in pay due to exceptional performance	D—Technique in which appraisees list activities they want to accomplish and appraisers mark what apraisees accomplished	D—Method in which experts submit initial predictions that are collected and then submit revised predictions after viewing the initial collection	D—Act focusing on gender discrimination among identical jobs
E—Violent verbal or physical attack	E—Process of developing new and unique ideas	E—Record of the history of an employee or patient used for analysis	E—Federal department that developed O*NET	E—Worker in company who pays half of Social Security costs

Definition Matrix Game 18 Continued—A Through E Words II

A	*B*	*C*	*D*	*E*
F—Leading society involved With training and development	F—Example would be hiring only females to be locker room attendants	F—Type of validity in which the predictive and criterion data are collected simultaneously	F—Minor violation of OSHA rules	F—Programs that take care of workers' elderly parents
G—Reduction of staff without replacing retirees	G—Type of leave employees receive due to the death of a relative	G—Validity focusing on matching test difficulty with job difficulty	G—Intentional unfair treatment of minority groups	G—Negotiation advantages from knowing the subject matter well
H—Thirty percent of these are needed to get union recognition moving	H—Examples include Social Security, vacation, and health insurance	H—Intensive written analysis of a company	H—Automatic payment of union dues	H—Learning through active participation in projects
I—Type of reliability in which test 1 is given at time 1 but a similar test is given at time 2	I—Science that deals with human actions	I—Group compared to the experimental group that receives no training	I—Type of thinking in which multiple ideas are created	I—One who starts a new business
J—Trial performance	J—Action in response to the environment	J—Index measuring the change in the cost of a market basket of goods	J—Study of population characteristics	J—Commission in charge of enforcing Title VII

Answer Matrix Game 18—A Through E Words II

A	*B*	*C*	*D*	*E*
A—Ability	A—Banding	A—Closed shop	A—Database	A—Experimental group
B—Ad hoc arbitrator	B—Behaviorally anchored rating scale	B—Correlation	B—Decentralization	B—Executive order
C—Agency shop	C—Blue collar workers	C—Criterion-oriented validity	C—Discriminant analysis	C—Essay test
D—Andragogy theory	D—Bonus	D—Checklist method	D—Delphi Method	D—Equal Pay Act
E—Assault	E—Brainstorming	E—Case history	E—Department of Labor	E—Employee
F—American Society for Training and Development	F—Bona fide occupational qualification	F—Concurrent validity	F—De minimus	F—Elder care
G—Attrition	G—Bereavement leave	G—Content Validity	G—Discrimination	G—Expert power
H—Authorization card	H—Benefits	H—Case study	H—Dues check off	H—Experiential learning
I—Alternate form reliability	I—Behavioral science	I—Control group	I—Divergent thinking	I—Entrepreneur
J—Audition	J—Behavior	J—Cost of Living Index or Consumer Price Index	J—Demographics	J—Equal Employment Opportunity Commission

Definition Matrix Game 19—F Through J Words I

F	*G*	*H*	*I*	*J*
A—Federal agency That keeps a list of arbitrators	A—Generation born roughly from 1965 to 1979	A—Performance appraisal error in which one good characteristic of a person overshadows every other characteristic	A—Strike stoppage technique banned by the Norris LaGuardia Act	A—"Window" associated with known to self and known to others
B—Statistical technique that identifies a few main factors associated with many variables	B—Generation born roughly from 1980 to 1999	B—Statistical guess to explain observed facts	B—European standardization system for quality	B—Approach to receive raw materials right before they are needed to reduce stockpiles
C—Federal publication containing regulations and laws	C—Court case that banned tests that have adverse impact unless they are job related	C—Two of six of these personality dimensions include concrete thinking and social interaction	C—Most common immigration form	C—Legal requirement to be on a jury
D—Policy protecting pregnant women from exposure to teratogens	D—Pay grade exception in which pay is below the pay grade	D—Explicit photographs in an office could help create this type of sexual harassment	D—I9 Form comes from this law	D—Businesses working together to create a new product
E—Requirement authorizing pension administrators to carefully invest in pension funds	E—Early retirement incentive for older employee that may involve a full pension	E—Domestic security law stemming from September 11, 2001 incident	E—Fun activity used to open meetings and introduce people to each other	E—Department of Labor free service connecting job applicants with companies

Definition Matrix Game 19 Continued—F Through J Words I

F	*G*	*H*	*I*	*J*
F—Job evaluation method that is a job to job comparison and quantitative	F—Incentive to keep key employees by removing a large benefit if the employee leaves	F—Period of time executives must keep their stock options	F—Equity within equity theory focusing on job evaluation	F—Companies rent a location for a day to recruit job candidates
G—Example includes getting a choice to work from 8 to 5 or 6 to 3	G—Companies that organize in multiple countries	G—Example includes employees who are 5 percent owners according to the Tax Reform Act of 1986	G—Rate of price increases	G—Training method In which employees move to several jobs to get diversified experience
H—Reinforcement schedule where you get rewarded every three times you move a device	H—Group that thinks the infallible leader is always right despite contradictory evidence	H—Taking over a company by making a ridiculously high bid for its stock	H—Example of this includes a German transferred to the U. S. To work for the U. S. company	H—Selection technique in which an employee is measured and observed while doing the job
I—Reinforcement schedule where you get rewarded once every three periods	I—Clause stating that companies must maintain a safe workplace beyond OSHA rules	I—Occasionally "renting" a cubicle while basing most work outside the company	I—Private corporate computer network	I—Federal government uses this general category of job evaluation method
J—An example of this includes a drug test incorrectly affirming that an employee is on drugs	J—Direction your company plans to go	J—Court ruling stating that psychological damage need not be proved in sexual harassment	J—Financial enticement to increase productivity	J—In a discharge, this is a fair and consistent enforcement of rules

Answer Matrix Game 19—F Through J Words I

F	*G*	*H*	*I*	*J*
A—Federal Mediation & Conciliation Service	A—Generation X	A—Halo error	A—Injunction	A—Johari Window
B—Factor analysis	B—Generation Y	B—Hypothesis	B—ISO 9000	B—Just in time
C—Federal Register	C—Griggs vs. Duke Power	C—Holland's personality dimensions	C—I9	C—Jury duty
D—Fetal protection policy	D—Green circle	D—Hostile environment	D—Immigration Control Act	D—Joint venture
E—Fiduciary responsibility	E—Golden handshake	E—Homeland Security Act	E—Icebreaker	E—Job Service
F—Factor comparison	F—Golden handcuffs	F—Holding period	F—Internal equity	F—Job fair
G—Flextime	G—Global corporation	G—Highly compensated employee	G—Inflation	G—Job rotation
H—Fixed ratio	H—Groupthink	H—Hostile takeover	H—Inpatriate	H—Job sampling
I—Fixed interval	I—General duty clause	I—Hoteling	I— Intranet	I—Job classification
J—False positive	J—Goal	J—Harris v. Forklift Systems	J—Incentive	J—Just cause

Definition Matrix Game 20—F Through J Words II

F	*G*	*H*	*I*	*J*
A—Organizational structure arranged by business function	A—Barrier women face preventing them from moving into management	A—Test used to investigate truthfulness of a job candidate	A—In Expectancy theory, if you do well, you will be paid	A—Method to determine pay by focusing on the market
B—Example is the choice of arriving at 6, leaving at 3 or arriving at 8 and leaving at 5	B—Federal government's job classification system	B—Pay allowance for expatriates associated with shelter	B—Assessment center exercise focusing on the prioritization of various memos	B—Giving employees more tasks at the same job level
C—Tax free money used for health care expenses	C—HR manager who covers all aspects of HR	C—Magazine produced by SHRM	C—Consistency among raters rating the same person	C—Giving workers more decision-making responsibilities
D—Unfair labor practice in which workers are hired to do little or nothing	D—Vesting schedule that begins with 20% vesting at year 3	D—Employee assets of an organization	D—Gain sharing program where workers earn money from savings coming producing in a shorter-than-expected time	D—Moving workers from one job to another to provide more training
E—Third party neutral who makes a ruling that is nonbinding	E—Example of this scale is a 1 being poor and a 5 being excellent	E—Workers who are paid for each 60 minute period	E—Cognitive ability measure where average is 100	E—Set of related tasks and duties

Definition Matrix Game 20 Continued—F Through J Words II

F	*G*	*H*	*I*	*J*
F—Type of validity based on appearances alone	F—Incentive program where groups of employees share gains from the company	F—Graph showing a frequency distribution via varying rectangles	F—University student gaining practical, supervised experience in a company	F—Fair and correct reason to discharge or discipline employees
G—Program that allows employees benefit choices	G—Doctor who controls which specialists a patient may use in an HMO	G—Managed care system that involves copayments	G—Union that has at least one local in another country	G—Taking a full-time job and dividing it in half
H—Example of this is requiring 10% A's and 90% F's	H—Type of bargaining where both sides are fair and open	H—Condition of being sound in mind and body	H—Meeting between employer and job candidate to discuss qualifications	H—Part of a job description that includes education, experience, and working conditions
I—Extra money given to expatriates just for going overseas	I—Process to resolve differences in a company	I—Performance appraisal error in which an employee is rated low because of one characteristic	I—Questionnaire that investigates what an employee interests and values	I—Label or name given to a job
J—Another name for the 80 percent rule	J—Difference between male and female pay for the same job	J—Herzberg factors that dissatisfy if you don't have enough	J—All types of equipment such as computers used for training	J—Employee's feelings about a job

Answer Matrix Game 20—F Through J Words II

F	*G*	*H*	*I*	*J*
A—Functional structure	A—Glass ceiling	A—Honesty test	A—Instrumentality	A—Job pricing method
B—Flextime	B—General Schedule	B—Housing allowance	B—Inbasket	B—Job enlargement
C—Flexible spending account	C—Generalist	C—HR Magazine	C—Interrater reliability	C—Job enrichment
D—Featherbedding	D—Graded vesting	D—Human capital	D—Improshare	D—Job rotation
E—Fact finder	E—Graphic rating scale	E—Hourly workers	E—IQ	E—Job
F—Face validity	F—Gain sharing	F—Histogram	F—Intern	F—Just cause
G—Flexible benefits	G—Gatekeeper	G—Health Maintenance Organization	G—International union	G—Job sharing or splitting
H—Forced distribution	H—Good faith bargaining	H—Healthy	H—Interview	H—Job specifications
I—Foreign service premium	I—Grievance procedure	I—Horn error	I—Interest inventory or test	I—Job title
J—Four fifths rule	J—Gender gap	J—Hygiene factors	J—Instructional technology	J—Job satisfaction

Definition Matrix Game 21—K Through O Words I

K	*L*	*M*	*N*	*O*
A—His work includes reaction, learning, behavior, and results	A—Pay policy in which a company is above the market for All of its jobs	A—Statistic associated with the most frequent occurrence	A—Trade agreement between the U. S., Canada, and Mexico eliminating tariff barriers	A—Federal agency enforcing Executive Orders and Affirmative Action
B—Top employees in the company	B—Pay policy in which a company is below the market for all of its jobs	B—Higher pay based on performance appraisal scores	B—Negotiation in which both sides can win	B—Developing organizational strategy to boost its performance
C—Benchmark bob	C—Pay policy where low level jobs get higher-than-market pay. Opposite for high level jobs	C—Pay set via salary surveys	C—Act that banned injunctions and yellow-dog contracts	C—Chart showing the employment hierarchies in an organization
D—Shape of a frequency distribution	D—Process of obtaining information through training	D—This grid includes (9, 1) and (1, 9) jobs	D—Reinforcement technique involving the removal of inhospitable conditions	D—Nonexempt employees must be paid time and a half for this
E—Computers placed in common areas to provide benefits information	E—Medical condition keeping an employee out of work for more than six months	E—Public sector unions negotiating with several levels of government	E—Top of the AFL-CIO organizational chart	E—Training in which you teach new employees about the company

Definition Matrix Game 21 Continued—K Through O Words I

K	*L*	*M*	*N*	*O*
F—Ideas and facts that employees have that helps them solve problems	F—Pay policy in which lower level jobs are paid below the market and high level jobs are paid above the market	F—Increased revenue coming from an additional unit of output	F—Example of this is when a convicted murderer gets hired by a school district	F—Type of training when employees are instructed while they work
G—Tax deductible pension for self-employed individuals	G—A contract by which an employee is provided to a company for a specified term	G—Exclusive ownership of an industry	G—Policy on hiring relatives	G—Department of Labor guide providing labor market projections for numerous jobs
H—Study of body movements	H—Rule of conduct recognized as binding by courts	H—American awards to promote quality based on rigorous on-site reviews of operations	H—Adding points to an employment test due to some personal characteristic	H—A person assigned to hear employee complaints and ethics violations
I—Pay based on knowledge obtained	I—Training technique in which real current corporate problems are incorporated	I—Company expanding its markets overseas by using its local resources	I—Group meeting where several experts get together to work on a problem	I—This occurs when side by side pay grades share pay ranges
J—Japanese concept involving everyone to improve production	J—Document designating how doctors and family will care for terminally ill patient	J—Curve based on years since last degree and salary	J—To meet in order to arrive at a settlement	J—Leadership in which a small group maintains control

Answer Matrix Game 21—K Through O Words I

K	*L*	*M*	*N*	*O*
A—Kirkpatrick	A—Lead policy	A—Mode	A—North American Free Trade Agreement	A—Office of Federal Contract Compliance Programs
B—Key employees	B—Lag policy	B—Merit pay	B—Non zero-sum game	B—Organizational development
C—Key job	C—Lead-lag policy	C—Market pricing	C—Norris LaGuardia Act	C—Organization chart
D—Kurtosis	D—Learning	D—Managerial Grid	D—Negative reinforcement	D—Overtime
E—Kiosk	E—Long-term disability	E—Multilateral bargaining	E—National convention	E—Orientation
F—Knowledge	F—Lag-lead policy	F— Marginal revenue	F—Negligent hiring	F—On-the-job training
G—Keogh plan	G—Leasing	G—Monopoly	G—Nepotism	G—Occupational Outlook Handbook
H—Kinesics	H—Law	H—Malcolm Baldrige Awards	H—Norming	H—Ombudsman
I—Knowledge based pay	I—Live or living case	I—Multinational corporation	I—Nominal group method	I—Overlap
J—Kalzen	J—Living will	J—Maturity curve	J—Negotiate	J—Oligarchy

Definition Matrix Game 22—K Through O Words II

K	*L*	*M*	*N*	*O*
A—Benchmark job	A—Polygraph	A—Example of this is an HMO	A—Job interview in which the candidate is in charge of most of the conversation	A—Physically looking at what an employee does
B—Author who developed four levels of training evaluation	B—Defined periods of life	B—Person who supervises others	B—This Wagner Act board certifies representation elections	B—What OWBPA stands for
C—Common employee area consisting of computers allowing them to gain information about their benefits	C—Discourse in front of a class	C—Statistical analysis that shows probable employment movement patterns based gender and other factors	C—Employee who is subject to the Fair Labor Standard Act	C—Department of Labor's replacement for the Dictionary of Occupational Titles
D—Important words placed in resumes to alert companies (through their scanners) of a candidate's qualifications	D—Publishing scandalous falsehoods about a person	D—Negotiations where a mediator could turn into an arbitrator	D—Type of organization whose employees can use 203(b) plans	D—Hours in which off-duty workers must remain available To work
E—Workers who do mostly intellectual work	E—Relationships between unions and management protected by labor laws	E—Federal health insurance program for those 65 or older or some disabled under 65	E—Pension plan not following IRS rules and not getting favorable tax incentives	E—Shop where there is no union

Definition Matrix Game 22 Continued—K Through O Words II

K	*L*	*M*	*N*	*O*
F—This job information collection activity leads to job descriptions	F—Discharge due to corporate financial problems	F—Emotional well-being	F—Asking for more after negotiations are over	F—Skinner's conditioning idea to use reinforcement to support desired responses
G—Death due to working too hard according to this Japanese term	G—One who leads	G—Experienced employees who guide and counsel less experienced employees	G—Agreement not allowing employees to work with a competitor for a specified time	G—Usually the first training employees receive
H—Research on body language and facial expressions	H—Gaining knowledge	H—Lowest hourly pay allowed in a state	H—Maslow listed five levels of these	H—Graphical representation of the organizational structure
I—Abbreviation for keep it simple stupid	I—Paid or unpaid temporary absence from a company	I—Working a second job	I—Mediation organization formed by the Railway Labor Act	I—Company-supported program To help employees who are laid off
J—IRS-approved pension plan for self-employed individuals	J—OSHA requirement to shut down electrical equipment and include a tag about it	J—Psychological test with 16 personality types	J—Highest level association of arbitrators	J—Learning by doing a skill excessively

Answer Matrix Game 22—K Through O Words II

K	*L*	*M*	*N*	*O*
A—Key job	A—Lie detector	A—Managed care	A—Nondirective interview	A—Observation
B—Kirkpatrick	B—Life stages	B—Manager	B—National Labor Relations Board	B—Older Workers Benefits Protection Act
C—Kiosk	C—Lecture	C—Markov Chain	C—Nonexempt employee	C—O*Net
D—Keyword	D—Libel	D—Med-Arb	D—Nonprofit	D—On-call time
E—Knowledge worker	E—Labor relations	E—Medicare	E—Nonqualified pension	E—Open shop
F—Karoshi	F—Layoff	F—Mental health	F—Nibbling	F—Operant conditioning
G—Kurtosis	G—Leader	G—Mentor	G—Non-compete Agreement	G—Orientation
H—Kinesics	H—Learning	H—Minimum wage	H—Needs	H—Organization chart
I—KISS	I—Leave	I—Moonlighting	I—National Mediation Board	I—Outplacement
J—Keough plan	J—Lockout/tagout	J—Myers-Briggs type indicator	J—National Academy of Arbitrators	J—Over learning

Definition Matrix Game 23—P Through T Words I

P	*Q*	*R*	*S*	*T*
A— Ranking individuals two at a time	A—Contract in a right to work state that states you have to join a union, unless there is a law that states otherwise	A—Simplest job evaluation technique focusing on the order of jobs	A—Performance appraisal error based on how identical job applicant is to the recruiter	A—Point in negotiations that negotiators wish to go
B—Bargaining results in a related company are followed in another	B—"This for that" concept associated with sexual harassment	B—Transferring money from one account to another without being taxed	B—Point in negotiations that negotiators actually conclude	B—Frederick's piece rate plan that can provide either increasing or decreasing returns
C—In experimental designs, this is a group that receives unrelated training and is compared to a control group	C—Fifth of a pay grade	C—Lewin's stage of training involving attempts to establish new skills into employee behavior	C—Largest human resource management society in the world	C—Studies made famous By Frederick Taylor focusing on efficient production techniques
D—College graduates need two years of experience to take this certification exam	D—Malcolm Baldrige Awards focus on this in general	D—Point in negotiations that negotiators will not compromise further	D—SHRM certification exam for veteran HR experts	D—McGregor's theory that assumes employees are children grown larger
E—Security-related Act associated with September 11, 2001	E—Programs, procedures, and policies companies use to ensure high quality products	E—Stock plan in which employees have restrictions on the sale of stock	E—Type of interview in which the interviewer purposely adds tension	E—Systematic use of violence to intimidate a population

Definition Matrix Game 23 Continued—P Through T Words I

P	*Q*	*R*	*S*	*T*
F—An inventor's right to exclusively sell his or her invention	F—Paper instrument that includes questions that respondents answer	F—Labor act that includes the National Mediation Board	F—Interview in which the interview provides a case that the interviewee must respond To	F—Anything business owners use that they don't want competitors to know about
G—Type of reinforcement in which rewards result from exhibiting good behavior	G—Theory associated with the most efficient way to reduce standing in line	G—Practice where extra points are given to certain races on selection tests	G—Paying people above a pay grade for seniority purposes only	G—Coordinated approach to organizational quality improvement
H—In reinforcement theory, this is a method to reduce undesirable behavior	H—Example of this is to require three female employees for every four male employees	H—As an exception, pay above the pay grade due to merit, seniority, or other reasons	H—Type of learning curve that starts slow, accelerates, then tapers off	H—Type of budgeting In which the organizational leadership provides basic direction to subordinates
I—Clerical workers	I—Quarter of a pay grade	I—Kirkpatrick's most useful but most difficult to measure level of training evaluation	I—Maslow's need theory highest level	I—Chief title associated with the Civil Rights Act of 1964
J—Organization that insures pensions	J—Stock option or profit sharing plan that meets IRS requirements for tax advantages	J—Example of this is to install elevators so wheel chaired individuals can work	J—Highest court in the United States	J—Personal characteristic

Answer Matrix Game 23—P Through T Words I

P	*Q*	*R*	*S*	*T*
A—Paired comparison	A—Quasi union shop	A—Ranking method	A—Similar to me or same as me error	A—Target point
B—Pattern bargaining	B—Quid pro quo	B—Rollover	B—Settlement point	B—Taylor Plan
C—Placebo	C—Quintile	C—Refreezing	C—Society for Human Resource Management	C—Time and motion studies
D—Professional In Human Resources	D—Quality	D—Resistance point	D—Senior Professional in Human Resources	D—Theory X
E—Patriot Act	E—Quality control programs	E—Restricted stock plan	E—Stress interview	E—Terrorism
F—Patent	F—Questionnaire	F— Railway Labor Act	F—Situational interview	F—Trade secret
G—Positive reinforcement	G—Queuing theory	G—Race norming	G—Silver circle	G—Total Quality Management
H—Punishment	H—Quota	H—Red Circle	H—S shaped curve	H—Top down budgeting
I—Pink collar workers	I—Quartile	I—Results	I—Self actualization	I—Title VII
J—Pension Benefit Guarantee Corporation	J—Qualified plan	J—Reasonable accommodation	J—Supreme Court	J—Trait

Definition Matrix Game 24—P Through T Words II

P	*Q*	*R*	*S*	*T*
A—Bar graph showing relative magnitude of problems	A—Group of employees who meet regularly for an hour To discuss quality	A—Involves managing workforce size by decreasing or increasing it	A—Unstructured group training to change behavior	A—Wrongful act against a person with no breach of contract
B—Business in which co-owners work together	B—Programs designed to maintain high quality products	B—Acknowledgement of accomplishments	B—Illnesses caused by poor conditions in buildings	B—Instrument to determine how much was learned
C—Pay in which senior employees are paid similar to junior employees	C—Statistical waiting line theory	C—Reverse discrimination case associated with Bakke	C—Unauthorized strike in which employees cease work while at the plant	C—Conference over phone lines
D—Digital feedback containing audio and video files for downloading	D—Individual paralyzed below the neck	D—Written summary of job candidate's record	D—Example of this plan Is giving a worker $60 for completing a project regardless of time	D—Performance appraisal in which everyone An employee is involved with can rate him or her
E—Examples of these for executives include golf club memberships and cars	E—Research that uses non-quantitative Information	E—Characteristic an applicant must have to get a job	E—Example of this is making $20 for every 10 units produced	E—Collection of job elements found in a Job description

Definition Matrix Game 24 Continued—P Through T Words II

P	*Q*	*R*	*S*	*T*
F—What a post-test is compared to	F—Programs to improve worker job satisfaction	F—Incentive plan in which employees share the risk of losses	F—Interview with a sequence of prepared questions	F—Group of employees working together
G—Set of activities to compete a product	G—Experimental study completed in less than ideal conditions	G—Written standard of conduct	G—Way of collecting data of employee attitudes	G—Employees working in a company for a short, specified period
H—Expectations affecting future performance	H—This for that	H—Customary way to solve problems	H—Contract in which union leaders are paid off by management to stop a strike	H—Benefits given to non-executive employees in case of a merger
I—Pre-employment tests focusing on repetitive manual tasks	I—Deceptive practice In non-right-to-work states to announce a union shop requirement in a contract	I—Bonus incentive plan from the 1930's including suggestion systems and committees	I—Secret observation of employees	I—Quality of stating concepts one wishes or believe to be true, rather than the facts
J—Useful work employers get from employees	J—Written means of collecting data	J—The Bakke case involved in this type of discrimination	J—Plan for the replacement of managers	J—Assertive type of personality

Answer Matrix Game 24—P Through T Words II

P	*Q*	*R*	*S*	*T*
A—Pareto chart	A—Quality circle	A—Rightsizing	A—Sensitivity training	A—Tort
B—Partnership	B—Quality assurance	B—Recognition	B—Sick building syndrome	B—Test
C—Pay compression	C—Queuing theory	C—Regents of the U. of California vs. Bakke	C—Sit down strike	C—Teleconference
D—Podcast	D—Quadriplegic	D—Resume	D—Standard Hour Plan	D—360 Degree feedback
E—Perks	E—Qualitative research	E—Requirement	E—Straight piecework plan	E—Task
F—Pretest	F—Quality of work life	F—Risk sharing	F—Structured interview	F—Team
G—Project	G—Quasi experimental study	G—Rule	G—Survey	G—Temps or temporaries
H—Pygmallion effect	H—Quid pro quo	H—Rule of thumb	H—Sweetheart contract	H—Tin parachute
I—Psychomotor test	I—Quasi union shop	I—Rucker Plan	I—Surveillance	I—Truthiness
J—Productivity	J—Questionnaire	J—Reverse discrimination	J—Succession plan	J—Type A personality

Definition Matrix Game 25—Last Letters/Numbers I

U	*V*	*W*	*X, Y, or Z*	*Numbers*
A—Multivariable analysis analyzing the usefulness of a selection test	A—Risk assessment analyzing the probability of violent acts	A—Court case overruled by the Civil Rights Act of 1991	A—Agreement to restrict parties from bargaining on issues not previously negotiated in the contract for the life of the contract	A—Number of required benefits for practically all companies with employees
B—Comparison of the number of qualified minorities in a relevant market for a job to who is in your company in that job	B—Example of this Include face, concurrent, predictive, and construct	B—Formerly the American Compensation Association	B—Win-lose game	B—Number of people appointed on the national NLRB
C—Fayol's principle of having only one boss and not two	C—European tax in which each level of production is taxed	C—Salaried employees such as managers and professionals	C—Contract requiring no union membership	C—Minimum organization size to complete OSHA forms 300 and 301
D—Insufficient minorities hired based on the qualified minorities in the relevant markets	D—Second highest ranking union officer	D—Type of negotiation in which both sides can win	D—Budgeting in which the prior budget is not assumed to continue and discussions start from scratch	D—Minimum organization size for the Civil Rights Act of 1964
E—ADA-related term would occur if Braille menus would be required for all small restaurants	E—Simulation-based training	E—Programs to enhance employee health through exercise, diet, and lifestyle promotion	E—Axis related to job evaluation points in a pay structure	E—Minimum organization size for the Age Discrimination Act

Definition Matrix Game 25 Continued—Last Letters/Numbers I

U	*V*	*W*	*X, Y, or Z*	*Numbers*
F—Accommodations for handicapped individuals that are too severe for implementation	F—Reinforcement schedule that Is similar to a pop quiz	F—Unauthorized strike	F—Relaxation exercise associated with bodily or mental control	F—Under COBRA, number of months handicapped former employees can receive benefits
G—Review of health benefit packages	G—Reinforcement schedule that Is similar to a slot machine	G—Reporting illegal company activities to the government	G—Program designed to achieve no errors in production	G—Under COBRA, number of months spouses of deceased employees can receive benefits
H—Federal guidelines associated with analyzing the reliability, validity, and adverse impact of selection tests	H—Concepts that a company considers highly	H—Incorrectly firing an individual	H—Ratio of recruiting success at each step of the recruiting process	H—Minimum organization size for FMLA
I—This is what USERRA stands for	I—Act protecting the rights of Vietnam veterans	I—International - organization combining national union federations	I—Internet journal	I—Number of days warning required under the WARN Act
J—In this country, most economic strikers can legally lose their jobs for striking	J—Landrum Griffin Act requires that union leaders get to office by collecting the most number of these	J—German council consisting of management and union members to help improve production	J—Standard score	J—Minimum organization size for writing EEO-1 reports

Answer Matrix Game 25—Last Letters/Numbers I

U	*V*	*W*	*X, Y, or Z*	*Numbers*
A—Utility analysis	A—Vulnerability analysis	A—Wards Cove vs. Antonio	A—Zipper clause	A—3
B—Utilization analysis	B—Validity	B—WorldAtWork	B—Zero sum game	B—5
C—Unity of command	C—Value added tax	C—White-collar employees	C—Yellow dog contract	C—11
D—Underutilization	D—Vice president	D—Win-win	D—Zero based budgeting	D—15
E—Undue hardship	E—Vestibule training	E—Wellness programs	E—X axis	E—20
F—United Nations	F—Variable interval schedule	F—Wildcat strike	F—Yoga	F—29
G—Utilization review	G—Variable ratio schedule	G—Whistle blowing	G—Zero defects	G—36
H—Uniform Guidelines	H—Values	H—Wrongful discharge	H—Yield ratio	H—50
I—Uniformed Services Employment and Reemployment Rights Act	I—Vietnam Veterans Readjustment and Rehabilitation Act	I—World Labor Organization	I—Zine	I—60
J—United States	J—Votes	J—Work council	J—Z score	J—100

Definition Matrix Game 26—Last Letters/Numbers II

U	*V*	*W*	*X, Y, Z*	*Numbers*
A—Example of this is dominating or interfering with the formation of unions according to the Wagner Act	A—Giving the employee the right to receive a pension after a certain period	A—Discharge for an incorrect reason	A—Contract that states You will never join a union	A—Glass ceilings were discussed in the Civil Rights Act of this year
B—These Guidelines recommend validity, reliability, and adverse impact analysis of selection tests	B—Sense of where a company wants to go in the long-term	B—Management tactic to create plant by plant competition for jobs to seek union concessions	B—Popular Internet search engine	B—Percent of employees needing to sign authorization cards
C—Behaviors that cause accidents	C—Work team linked through computers	C—What Marshall vs. Barlows allows companies to obtain	C—Young, upwardly mobile urban professionals	C—Number of right to work states
D—Working conditions that cause accidents	D—Distance training In which students are linked via monitors	D—Workers who earn this must be paid time and a half for overtime	D—An acute viral disease found In tropical regions and transmitted by mosquito	D—Number of IRS rules concerning definition of independent contractors
E—According to Lewin, this occurs when barriers to new knowledge are eliminated	E—Extra points given to veterans in selection tests	E—Laying off all of the workforce for part of the day to save money	E—Type of clause that helps end debate in union management relationships	E—Minimum number of years records of employee exposure to toxins must be kept

Definition Matrix Game 26 Continued—Last Letters/Numbers II

U	*V*	*W*	*X, Y, or Z*	*Numbers*
F—This occurs when minority groups are inadequately represented in a company	F—Corporate production arrangement in which harvesting, manufacturing, and selling are all done within the company	F—One of the main three required benefits	F—Abbreviation for the generation born from about 1964 to 1979	F—Maximum number of years ERISA allows to reach 100% vesting using cliff vesting
G—Centralized national labor union most associated with car makers	G—Pay based on any kind of performance	G—Salaried employees not involved with manual labor	G—Male chromosome	G—Maximum number of years ERISA allows to reach 100% vesting using graded vesting
H—In construction companies, this type of shop requires employees to join a union after seven days	H—Trade and paraprofessional education provided at colleges	H—Strike	H—Win-lose game	H—Common multiplier used to calculate annual pay based on hourly pay
I—Social Security, Workers' Compensation and this are the three major required benefits	I—Equity provided to new businesses based on projected growth research	I—Employers provide this form to report tax liabilities for withholding	I—Ratio of what a company yields from each step in the recruiting process	I—Number of personalities in Holland's typology
J—This occurs when reasonable accommodations for handicapped individuals cannot legally be met	J—Scheduled period away from work for rest and relaxation	J—Next typical progressive discipline step after the oral warning	J—Budgeting by starting from scratch	J—Number of years a college graduate must have exempt HR experience to qualify for PHR

Answer Matrix Game 26—Last Letters/Numbers II

U	*V*	*W*	*X, Y, Z*	*Numbers*
A—Unfair labor practices	A—Vesting	A—Wrongful discharge	A—Yellow dog contract	A—1991
B—Uniform Guidelines	B—Vision	B—Whipsawing	B—Yahoo	B—30
C—Unsafe acts	C—Virtual team	C—Warrant	C—Yuppie	C—22
D—Unsafe conditions	D—Video conference	D—Wage	D—Yellow fever	D—20
E—Unfreezing	E—Veterans' preference	E—Work sharing	E—Zipper clause	E—30
F—Underutilization	F—Vertical integration	F—Workers' Compensation	F—Xer	F—5
G—United Auto Workers	G—Variable pay or compensation	G—White collar workers	G—XY chromosomes	G—7
H—Union shop	H—Vocational education	H—Walkout	H—Zero sum game	H—2080
I—Unemployment Insurance	I—Venture capital	I—W-4 Forms	I—Yield ratio	I—6
J—Undue hardship	J—Vacation	J—Written warning	J—Zero base budgeting	J—2

Definition Matrix Game 27—Laws

Discrimination I	*Employee and Labor Relations*	*Compensation and Benefits*	*Other*	*Other II*
A—Covers discrimination in gender, race, national origin, color, and religion	A—Protects labor unions from unfair labor practices of management	A—Identical jobs should be paid equally regardless of the gender of the jobholder	A—Act that contains a general duty clause and involves Form 301	A—Allows federal enforcement agencies added options to deal with terrorism
B—Covers discrimination associated with childbirth and treats it as any temporary disability	B—Authorizes sixty day notifications for major plant closings	B—Establishes minimum wage and overtime rules	B—Established government insurance program covering retirement, survivors, disability and Medicare benefits	B—Gives authors control over how original materials can be duplicated
C—Law associated with the age 40 and above	C—Allows right-to-work laws to be established in states	C—Associated with care of parents and the phrase "up to twelve weeks"	C—Allows employees to review the employer's records on them and seek damages for inappropriate use	C—Limits the payout limits of qualified pension programs
D—Law for the private sector involving reasonable accommodation and undue hardship	D—Bans yellow dog contracts and certain types of injunctions	D—What HIPAA stands for	D—Similar to OSHA but in the underground and surface mining industries	D—Associated with mental health benefit and medical benefit parity
E—Prohibits federal contractors from discrimination against veterans of the Vietnam War	E—Protects union members from unfair union leadership practices	E—Established managed care centers that allow co-payments	E—Requires public construction workers such as mechanics be paid the prevailing wage	E—Replaced the Job Training Partnership Act

Definition Matrix Game 27 Continued—Laws

Discri-mination I	*Employee and Labor Relations*	*Compen-sation and Benefits*	*Other*	*Other II*
F—Establishes penalties for hiring illegal aliens and involves I-9 forms	F—Does not allow U. S. postal workers to strike	F—Key terms include vesting, fiduciary responsibility, vesting, PBGC, and portability	F—Extends Davis Bacon's prevailing wage concept to government contracts	F—Wages are to be calculated based on an 8 hour day and 40 hour work week.
G—Makes race norming illegal	G—Does not allow federal workers to strike	G—Amends the ADEA by including employee benefit programs for older workers	G—Requires federal contractors with $100k contracts to certify a drug-free workplace	G—Gives all people, regardless of age, race, and national origin, similar contractual rights as "white citizens"
H—ADA equivalent for federal contractors with contracts of $10,000 or more	H—Established the National Mediation Board for railway and airline industry labor relations	H—Health insurance law associated with a maximum 102 percent premium	H—Prohibits most employees from mandatory polygraph testing	H—Prevents government entities from requiring disclosure of electronic communications from a provider without proper procedures
I—Allows service credit and benefit continuation for workers on active military duty	I—Protects federal employees who disclose corruption in government expenditures	I—Introduced 401(k)	I—Executives may not mislead the public about the company's finances	I—Allows federal employees to participate in political activities
J—Discrimination legislation should apply to Congressional employees	J—Requires that certain chemicals be safety tested	J—Enhances the accuracy of consumers' financial information and helps fight identity theft	J—Provided tax exclusions for employer provided tuition assistance	J—Permits employees over 50 to pay catch up contributions for their pension plans

Answer Matrix Game 27—Laws

Discrimination	*Employee and Labor Relations*	*Compensation and Benefits*	*Other*	*Other II*
A—Civil Rights Act of 1964	A—Wagner (National Labor Relations) Act	A—Equal Pay Act	A—Occupational Safety and Health Act	A—USA Patriot Act
B—Pregnancy Discrimination Act	B—Worker Adjustment and Retraining Notification Act	B—Fair Labor Standards Act	B—Social Security Act	B—Copyright Act
C—Age Discrimination in Employment Act	C—Taft-Hartley (Labor-Management Relations) Act	C—Family and Medical Leave Act	C—Privacy Act	C—Omnibus Budget Reconciliation Act
D—Americans With Disabilities Act	D—Norris-LaGuardia Act	D—Health Insurance Portability and Accountability Act	D—Mining Safety and Health Act	D—Mental Health Parity Act
E—Vietnam Era Veterans' Readjustment Assistance Act	E—Landrum-Griffin	E—Health Maintenance Organization Act	E—Davis Bacon Act	E—Workforce Development Act
F—Immigration Reform and Control Act	F—Postal Reorganization Act	F—Employee Retirement Income Security Act	F—Walsh-Healy Public Contracts Act	F—Work Hours Act
G—Civil Rights Act of 1991	G—Civil Service Reform Act	G—Older Workers Benefit Protection Act	G—Drug-Free Workplace Act	G—Civil Rights Act of 1866
H—Rehabilitation Act	H—Railway Labor Act	H—COBRA	H—Polygraph Protection Act	H—Electronic Communications Privacy Act
I—USERRA	I—Whistleblower Protection Act	I—Revenue Act	I—Sarbanes-Oxley Act	I—Hatch Act
J—Congressional Accountability Act	J—Toxic Substance Control Act	J—Fair and Accurate Credit Transactions Act	J—Small Business Job Protection Act	J—Economic Growth and Tax Relief Reconciliation Act

Definition Matrix Game 28—Court Cases

Discri-mination I	*Discrim-ination II*	*Discrim-ination III*	*Other Cases I*	*Other Cases II*
A—It is not enough to show discriminatory intent if the - employment measure results in disparate impact	A—Established burden of proof for plaintiffs and defendants in discriminations cases	A—All selection procedures could be subject to adverse impact analysis	A—First court case declaring unions to be not an illegal constraint of trade	A—In certain cases, employers can unilaterally void provisions of a labor contract due to bankruptcy
B—Employment requirements must be job related according to this 1975 act. Uniform Guidelines of Selection Procedures were enhanced.	B—Employer has the burden of proof to show that an employment requirement is job related	B—Established the bottom line concept whereby the focus should be on the nondiscriminatory effect of the whole selection process rather than individual components	B—OSHA inspectors must produce a warrant if requested by the employer	B—Three Supreme Court cases affirming the legal support for arbitration
C—Even if an employment test has adverse impact, it is legal if it is job related	C—1988 case in which firefighters have a right to sue for reverse discrimination	C—If the employer's reason for firing is false, a jury may decide if discrimination is the reason	C—Employers are not allowed to form action committees that are labor organizations dominated by the employer	C—OSHA inspectors do not have to show probable cause to get a warrant

Definition Matrix Game 28 Continued—Court Cases

Discrimination I	*Discrimination II*	*Discrimination III*	*Other Cases I*	*Other Cases II*
D—The plaintiff does not have to prove psychological distress to file under the Civil Rights Act of 1964	D—Racial quotas are illegal especially where insufficient documentation of discrimination is provided	D—Evidence of illegal activities after termination (after acquired evidence) will not keep employers from being liable for discrimination	D—Employers are not allowed to circumvent unions through their own team processes	D—Pay differences of jobs that are different may indicate discrimination under Title VII
E—Race may be used as an admissions consideration in universities	E—In constructive discharge cases, an employer's defense may center on the employee's inadequate opportunity to solve the problem before the employee quit	E—If an official discrimination act leads to constructive discharge, an affirmative defense does not apply in which the employer takes reasonable care to prevent or correct harassment	E—Union employees have a right to a union representative in dealing with investigatory interviews	E—Upheld the use of market data for pay differences for different jobs

Definition Matrix Game 28 Continued—Court Cases

Discrimination I	*Discrimination II*	*Discrimination III*	*Other Cases I*	*Other Cases II*
F—Affirmative action plans are legal if they include voluntary quotas that both the union and the company have agreed upon	F—To recover from punitive damages, the employee must prove that the employer's actions were with reckless indifference. Outrageous conduct need not be proved	F—If an official discrimination act does not lead to changes in employment status, an affirmative defense does apply in which the employer takes reasonable care to prevent and correct harassment	F—Pre-hire employment applications requiring all disputes be settled by arbitration is enforceable by the Federal Arbitration Act	F—Under the Equal Pay Act, the equal work standard requires jobs to be substantially but not identically equal
G—There is a state interest to justify race in university admissions as long is admissions policies are narrowly tailored to achieve goals	G—Younger workers are not protected by the Age Discrimination in Employment Act	G—Gender may be considered in employment situations if affirmative action plans include no quotas	G—Companies must provide a list of eligible voters in representation elections within seven days of the request	G—Companies should use job related criteria for evaluating employee work performance to be used for promotions and discharges to reduce discrimination
H—Plaintiffs must show a prima facie case of disparate treatment in discrimination cases first	H—People with contagious diseases can be covered by the Rehabilitation Act of 1973	H—In discrimination cases, plaintiffs must prove they are minorities, applied and were rejected for a job, and the job remained open for people with equal or lesser qualifications	H—Former employees must be given the same protection from retaliation as employees and job applicants under Title VII	H—Appeals court decision declaring the State of Washington need not correct (comparable worth) disparity in pay among men and women

Definition Matrix Game 28 Continued—Court Cases

Discrimination I	*Discrimination II*	*Discrimination III*	*Other Cases I*	*Other Cases II*
I—Sexual harassment is a violation of the Civil Rights Act of 1964	I—Individuals with HIV and AIDS are covered by the ADA	I—Supreme Court case largely overturned by the Civil Rights Act of 1991	I—Gays and lesbians are entitled to equal rights, as opposed to special rights minorities and women receive through affirmative action	I—Affirmative action programs should not be used to layoff senior white employees in order to keep junior black employees
J—Same sex harassment is sexual harassment under Title VII	J—Person may not have a disability of the condition is corrected or controlled by medication or other applications	J—Anyone with an employment relationship with a business may use employment discrimination laws	J—Salting in which a worker is a company employee and a paid union organizer is legal	J—Employees denied rightful benefits under ERISA can seek remedies in the federal courts

Answer Matrix Game 28—Court Cases

Discri-mination I	*Discri-mination II*	*Discri-mination III*	*Other Cases I*	*Other Cases II*
A—Griggs vs. Duke Power	A—McDonnell Douglas vs. Green	A—Watson vs. Fort Worth Bank and Trust	A—Commonwealth vs. Hunt	A—NLRB vs. Bildisco & Bildisco
B—Albamarle vs. Moody	B—Griggs vs. Duke Power	B—Connecticut vs. Teal	B—Marshall vs. Barlows	B—Steelworkers' Trilogy
C—Washington vs. Davis	C—Martin vs Wilks	C—St. Mary's Honor Center vs. Hicks	C—Electromation Inc.vs. NLRB	C—Marshall vs. Barlows
D—Harris vs. Forklift Systems	D—City of Richmond vs. J. A. Croson Company	D—McKennon vs. Nashville Banner Publishing Company	D—E. I Dupont de Nemours & Company vs. NLRB	D—Gunther vs. County of Washington
E—Regents of the University of California vs. Bakke	E—Pennsylvania State Police vs. Suders	E—Pennsylvania State Police vs. Suders	E—NLRB vs. J. Weingarten	E—Spaulding vs. University of Washington
F—United Steelworkers vs. Weber	F—Kolstad vs. American Dental Association	F—Faragher vs. City of Boca Raton	F—Circuit City Stores vs. Adams	F—Schultz vs. Wheaton Glass
G—Grutter vs. Bollinger or Gratz vs. Bollinger	G—General Dynamics Land Systems vs. Cline	G—Johnson vs. Santa Clara County Transportation Agency	G— NLRB vs. Excelsior Underwear Inc.	G—Brito vs. Zia
H—McDonnell Douglas vs. Green	H—School Board of Nassau vs. Arline	H—McDonnell Douglas vs. Green	H—Robinson vs. Shell Oil Company	H—AFSCME vs. State of Washington
I—Meritor Savings Bank vs. Vinson	I—Bragdon vs. Abbott	I—Ward's Cove vs. Antonio	I—Romer vs. Evans	I—Firefighters vs. Stotts
J—Oncale vs. Sundowner Offshore Service	J—United States vs. Sutton	J—Walters vs. Metropolitan Educational Enterprises	J—Town and Country Electric vs. NLRB	J—Varity Corporation vs. Howe

Definition Matrix Game 29—Miscellaneous

Computers	*International*	*Ethics*	*Alternate Forms of Work*	*Miscella-neous*
A—A database with relevant HR information	A—Person who is sent overseas by a multinational corporation	A—Basic reason for a company's existence	A—On a small farm, these individuals do not get OSHA protection	A—Union of two corporations
B—Software used to surf the Web	B—A company that expands its domestic market to an international market	B—Involve why and how one ought to act	B—Downsizing everyone for a few hours each day	B—Weather-related problems that affect employees that management has no control over
C—Worldwide network of computer networks	C—Example of this person includes a German working in Germany for an American company	C—Document that shows conduct that guides management and employee behavior beyond what is required by law	C—Splitting a full time job into two part time jobs	C—Public sector laws that ensure that information is made public
D—Satellite-based system useful for finding locations of employees	D—Example of this person includes a German working in France for an American company	D—Person who investigates ethics complaints in a company	D—Individuals who pay 100% of their Social Security who work in a company	D—Career route followed by women who choose to be mothers
E—Law that restricts e-mail monitoring	E—European market established by the Maastricht Treaty	E—Involve a system of rules that stabilize social institutions	E—Part-time, temporary, or contract worker	E—Stock plans providing stock or cash payments based on hypothetical investments

Definition Matrix Game 29 Continued—Miscellaneous

Computers	*International*	*Ethics*	*Alternate Forms of Work*	*Miscella-neous*
F—Blackboard and WebCt are examples of this	F—Organization that enforces trade rules over many nations	F—Person who reveals wrongdoing within an organization to the public	F—Someone who is working less than full-time	F—Point system that includes know how, problem solving and accountability
G—A program that translates another program into a form acceptable to the computer	G—Business that are closely linked to create new products	G—Principle considered desirable	G—Example of this is 3/36 and 4/48	G—Budgeting system that uses zero funding as a starting point rather than last year's funding levels
H—Any information in a form a computer can use	H—Extra money for an expatriate for working in a country with harsh living conditions	H—Order issued by the European Union	H—Example of this includes choosing to arrive work at 6am and leave at 3pm or arrive at 8am and leave at 5pm	H—Legal principle that maintains individuals should be protected from arbitrary and unfair treatment
I—Software in which data is organized in rows and columns on a screen.	I—Country with the largest population in the world	I—Hiring and firing employees for good reason, bad reason, or reason morally wrong	I—Working outside the company grounds via telephone or computer connection	I—Written policy concerning employee attire
J—Consist of silicon chips and an antenna that can transmit data to a wireless receiver, could one day be used to track everything	J—Along with the U. S., only other country without nationalized health insurance	J—Not completing what is required in a contract	J—Telecommuting in which most work is done outside the office but office space is "rented"	J—Rule of thumb ratio of human resource managers to employees in a typical company

Answer Matrix Game 29—Miscellaneous

Computers	*International*	*Ethics*	*Alternative Forms of Work*	*Miscella-neous*
A—Human resource information systems	A—Expatriate	A—Mission	A— Immediate family	A—Merger
B—Browser	B—Multinational corporation	B—Ethics	B—Work sharing	B—Acts of god
C—Internet	C—Local or host country national	C—Code of Ethics	C—Job sharing	C—Sunshine laws
D—Global Positioning Systems	D—Third country national	D—Ombudsman or ethics officer	D—Independent contractors	D—Mommy track
E—Electronic Communications Privacy Act	E—European Union	E—Law	E—Contingency worker	E—Phantom stock plans
F—E-learning systems or Web-based course management systems	F—World Trade Organization	F—Whistleblower	F—Part-time work	F—Hay System
G—Processor	G—Joint venture	G—Values	G—Compressed work week	G—Zero-based budgeting
H—Software	H—Hardship allowance	H—Directives	H—Flextime	H—Due process
I—Spreadsheet	I—China	I—Employment at will	I—Telecommuting	I—Dress code
J—RFID, radio frequency identification tags	J—South Africa	J—Breach of contract	J—Hoteling	J—1 to 100

Chapter Four

Brainstorming Games

PURPOSE

To help students brainstorm concepts to retrieve information for test questions for human resource certification exams. For example, in the SPHR exam, problem solving questions don't mention the laws or terms. To answer the questions, you must be able to retrieve appropriate terms and laws.

WAYS TO PLAY

Match the List

Version 1—One Player: With every topic shown in this chapter, come up with as many terms or laws as possible. If a term or law is matched on the list provided, a player receives two points. If a player states a term that is not on the list but still fits the topic, he or she gets one point.

Version 2—Two or More Players: Pick a topic. Have each player write down as many terms related to the topic. A player receives two points for each term that is matched on the list. A player receives one point for each term that fits the topics but is not in the list. The player with the most points wins.

Version 3—One or More Players: If the "Match The List" lists are used up, go to the previous chapter answer keys and try to match the lists there. Good luck on any "miscellaneous" topic.

Version 4—One or More Players: Again, if the "Match The List" lists are used up, create a list by grabbing a glossary from an HR textbook, Website, or other document and write down as many HR terms that start with the letter "A", "B", and so on. Get two points for matching the glossary term and one point for going beyond the glossary.

Unique Term

Version 1—Two or more players: Write down as many terms related to the topic. A player receives two points for each term that is matched on the list AND is unique to that player. A player receives one point for each term that fits the topics but is not on list AND is unique to that player. If a term is not unique to the player, the player receives no points.

Version 2—Two or more players: Do the same activity with any answer key list provided in the previous chapter's answer keys or in any glossary.

Avoid the List

Version 1—One or more players: Write down as many terms related to the topic. A player receives a point related to the topic that is NOT on any list in this chapter. Good luck. This game is really hard.

Version 2—One or more players: Tackle any answer key in the previous chapter or any glossary." A player receives a point related to the topic that is not on any list. Given the difficulty of this game, cheating might be acceptable by trying to find alternative choices on the Internet or other textbooks.

Ball Toss

Version 1—Three or more players: An HR study group might have covered some terms the previous day or week. When your study group returns the next day or week, have a person bring a ball that can be tossed. The ball could be a rolled up sheet of paper, racquetball, tennis ball, ping pong ball or anything else that is round and soft. Avoid bowling balls. When a player receives a ball thrown by another person, he or she must state a term that was covered and then define it. Then he or she passes it to the next victim—player.

Version 2—Three or more players: The first person mentions a term covered the previous day, tosses a round and soft ball to another person who has to define the term. That person then mentions another term and tosses the ball to the next victim who has to define the term and mention yet another term—and so on.

Stump the Band

Version 1—Two or more players: This is a twist of an old Tonight Show with Johnny Carson game. A player looks at a brainstorming list in this chapter and picks the three to five most difficult words that he or she thinks others in the group will not be able to define. The player gets a point for every word that cannot be defined by the group. Because there are no of the terms shown in the brainstorming chapter, check the Internet or a major textbook for the term.

Version 2—Two or more players: Grab a glossary from a textbook, certification study guide, or Website. Have each player take the three to five hardest words from a page and get a point for each word no one else gets.

BRAINSTORMING GAMES

Section A Strategy

Cultural Dimensions
Individualism versus collectivism, Indulgence versus restraint
Long-term versus short-term orientation
Masculinity versus femininity
Power distance
Uncertainty avoidance

International Workers
Expatriates
Frequent flyers
Inpatriates
Local nationals, Long-term workers
Parent-country nationals
Repatriates
Short-term workers
Third-country nationals
Virtual workers

Financial Measures
Debt, Dividend yield
Earnings per share, Earnings before interest and taxes, Economic margin,
Economic profit, Enterprise value
Gross margin, Gross profit
Market share, Market value added
Net profit
Price earnings ratio
Return on assets, Return on equity, Return on investment, Revenue growth, Revenue per employee
Shareholder value
Total shareholder return

Labor Forecasting Methods
Delphi technique
Econometric models
Flow analysis

Gap analysis
Job analysis
Managerial judgment
Nominal groups
Ratio analysis, Regression analysis
Scatter plot, Scenario forecasting, Simulations
Work study technique, Workforce analysis
Trend analysis, Turnover analysis

Strategic Planning Terminology
Action plans
Benchmarking
Concentration, Consolidation, Cost leadership
Data mining, Differentiation, Digital dashboard, Diversification
Expansion (geographic, product line)
Focuser
Growth
HR metrics, HR Scorecard
Integration (horizontal, vertical)
Objectives (long, medium, short)
Mission
Retrenchment
Stability
Strategy (corporate, business-level, divisional, functional), Strategy map, SWOT
Values, Vision

Section B Employment

Alternative Work Arrangements
Banking of hours
Compressed work week
Flextime
Leaves
Job sharing
Partial work year, Permanent part-time work, Phased retirement
Sabbatical
Telecommuting/flexplace
Work sharing

Anti-discrimination Laws

Age Discrimination in Employment, Americans with Disabilities Act (ADA), ADA Amendments
Civil Rights Act of 1866, Civil Rights Act of 1964, Civil Rights Act of 1991
Equal Pay
Genetic Information Nondiscrimination
Immigration Reform and Control
Lilly Ledbetter Fair Pay
Pregnancy Discrimination
Rehabilitation
Uniformed Services Employment and Reemployment Rights
Vietnam Veterans Readjustment Assistance

Discrimination Court Cases

Albemarle Paper vs. Moody
Brown vs. Board of Education
Dred Scott vs. Sanford
Faragher vs. City of Boca Raton
Griggs vs. Duke Power
Harris vs. Forklift Systems
McDonnell Douglas vs. Green, McKennon vs. Nashville Banner Publishing, Meritor Savings Bank vs. Vinson
Oncale vs. Sundowner Offshore Services
Regents of the University of California vs. Bakke
Spurlock v. United Airlines
St. Mary's Honor Center vs. Hicks
United Steelworkers vs. Weber
Washington vs. Davis, Wygant vs. Jackson Board of Education

Equal Employment Opportunity Terms

Adverse impact, Affirmative action, Alternative dispute resolution
Bona fide occupational qualification, Burden of proof, Business necessity
Discrimination, Disparate impact, Disparate treatment, Diversity
Eighty percent rule
Hostile environment
Protected class
Qualified individuals, Quid pro quo
Reasonable accommodation, Reverse discrimination
Sexual harassment

Teratogens
Undue hardship
Voluntary mediation

Interview Types
Behavioral, Breakfast
Case
Dinner
Face-to-face
Group
Informational
Lunch
Non-directive
Panel/committee
Situational, Stress
Telephone

Job Analysis Methods
Checklists, Critical incidents
Diaries
Interviews
Observation
Questionnaires
Technical conference
Videos
Work samples

Job Description Components
Action verbs
Date
Effort, Elastic clause, Essential job functions
Job competencies, Job title, Job level, Job specifications
Know how
Nonessential job functions
Pay
Responsibilities
Signatures, Skills
Tasks
Working conditions

Recruiting Methods—External

Associations
Billboards
Career fairs, Company website
Former employees
Internships
Job portals
Newspapers
Public employment agencies
Radio
Schools—colleges and universities, Social media
Television, Temporary agencies
Unions
Walk-ins

Recruiting Methods—Internal

E-mails
Job bidding, Job posting
Newsletters
Referrals
Promotions
Retired employees
Skill banks
Temps for permanent positions
Word of mouth

Reliability Analysis Types

Parallel
Split Half
Test-retest

Selection Tests

Ability, Age (not legal in most cases), Alcohol, Application form, Aptitude, Assessment centers
Background checks
Color (not legal), Credit history (not legal in most cases)
Drug
Gender (not legal except BFOQ), Genetic (not legal) Grades
Handshake, Handwriting, Honesty
Intelligence, Interest

Job knowledge
Medical (not legal)
National origin (not legal)
Personality, Polygraph (not legal in most cases), Psychomotor
Race (not legal), Reference checks
Veteran (legal in Federal and many state sectors)

Validity Analysis Types
Content, Construct, Concurrent
Predictive

Section C Development

Leadership Theories
Behavioral
Contingency (Fiedler)
Leadership Continuum (Tannenbaum and Schmidt)
Managerial Grid (Blake-Mouton)
Path Goal (House)
Situational leadership (Hersey-Blanchard)
Trait

Learning Curves
Decreasing
Increasing
Plateued
S-Shaped

Levels of Training Evaluation (in chronological order)
Reaction
Learning
Behavior
Results

Motivational Theories
Equity, Expectancy (Expectancy, Instrumentality, Valence)
Herzberg's Hygiene Theory
Maslow's Hierarchy of Needs, McClelland (need for achievement, affiliation, power)

Reinforcement
Theory X and Y

Performance Appraisal Errors
Bias
Central tendency, Contrast (order)
Falsehood, First impression
Gut feeling
Halo, Horn
Inconsistent questions
Lack of follow-up, Last impression (same as recency), Late evaluation, Leniency
Negative emphasis, Not knowing the job
One sided dialogue, Over evaluation
Poor interview (environment, time)
Recency (same as last impression)
Same as me, Snap judgments, Stereotypes

Performance Appraisal Methods
Alternation ranking
Behaviorally anchored rating scales, Behavioral expectation scales, Behavioral observation scales
Checklists, Critical incidents
Essays
Field review, Forced choice, Forced distribution
Graphic rating scales
Management by objectives
Paired comparison
Ranking, Records
360 degree

Training Methods
Apprenticeship, Audio conference, Audio-tapes
Behavioral modeling, Blended learning, Brainstorming
Cases, CD-ROM, Coaching, Computer conference, Consultants, Contests, Cross-training
Demonstrations, Discussions, Drills
Games
E-mail
Homework

Job enlargement, Job enrichment, Job instruction training, Job rotation
Learning portal, Lectures
Mentoring, Movies, Multimedia
On-the-job, One-to-one, Outdoor training
Programmed instruction
Question cards, Quizzes
Relocation, Role plays, Ropes course, Reading
Seminars, Sensitivity training, Simulations, Simulators
Text-only
Vestibule, Video conference, Virtual reality
Webinar

Section D Pay

Benefits Required By Federal and Many State Laws

Consolidated Omnibus Budget Reconciliation
Health Insurance via the Affordable Care Act
Leaves via the Family Medical Leave Act
Social Security
Unemployment Insurance
Workers' Compensation

Compensation and Benefits Laws

Age Discrimination in Employment
Black Lung Benefits
Civil Rights Act of 1964, Civil Rights Act of 1991, Consumer Credit Protection, Copeland
Davis-Bacon, Dodd-Frank Wall Street Reform and Consumer Protection
Employee Retirement Income Security, Energy Employees Occupational Illness Compensation Program
Fair Labor Standards, Federal Employees' Compensation
Lilly Ledbetter Fair Pay, Longshore and Harbor Workers' Compensation
McNamara-O'Hara Service Contract, Migrant and Seasonal Agricultural Worker Protection
Portal-to-Portal
Service Contract
Walsh-Healey

Defined Benefit Terms

Cliff vesting
Defined benefits, Disability retirement
Employee Retirement Income Security Act
Fiduciary responsibility, Formulas (terminal earnings, career earnings, dollar amount, percentage of contribution)
Graded vesting
Job Creation and Worker Assistance Act
Lump sum payment
Nonqualified pension plans, Normal retirement
Older Workers' Benefit Protection Act
Qualified pension plans
Pension Benefits Guarantee Corporation, Portability
Vesting

Defined Contribution Plans

Coverdell Education Savings Accounts
Employee stock ownership
529
457, 401(k), 403(b)
Individual retirement accounts (IRA)
Money purchase
Profit sharing
Rabbi trusts, Roth IRA
Savings Incentive Match Plan for Employees (SIMPLE), Simplified Employee Pension (SEP)
Thrift savings, Top hat

Job Evaluation Methods

Classification
Factor comparison
General Schedule
Hay method
Job classification, Job component method
Market pricing
Point-Factor
Ranking

Health Plans
Employee Assistance Programs, Exclusive Provider Organization
Flexible benefits plans, Flexible spending accounts
Health Maintenance Organization
Indemnity
Medical Savings Accounts, Minimum Premium Plan, Multiple Employer Welfare Arrangement
Physician-Hospital Organization, Point of Service, Preferred Provider Organization
Wellness Programs

Pay Structure Terms
Benchmark jobs, Broad banding
Comparable worth, Compa-ratio, Compensable factor
Grades, Gold circle, Green circle
Job analysis, Job descriptions, Job evaluation
Overlap
Market wage curve, Maximum, Midpoint, Minimum
Quartiles
Percentiles, Points, Pay compression, Pay range, Pay survey
Range spread, Red circle,
Silver circle
Two-tier

Section E Relations

Bargaining Topics—Illegal
Closed shop
Discriminatory treatment
Hot cargo clauses

Bargaining Topics—Mandatory
Bargaining unit work
Christmas bonus
Discipline, Discharge, Discounts, Drug testing, Dues check off
Employee security
Grievance procedure
Health insurance, Holidays, Hours of work, Housing
Insurance

Job duties, Job performance
Layoff, Leaves of absence, Longevity
Meals
No strike clause
Nondiscrimination
On call pay, Overtime pay
Pay, Pensions, Premium pay, Probationary period, Profit sharing plans, Promotions
Recall, Rest and lunch periods
Seniority, Severance pay, Shift differentials, Sick days, Subcontracting
Testing of employees, Training pay, Transfers, Tuition reimbursement
Union security
Vacancies
Wages, Workloads, Work schedules

Bargaining Topics—Permissible
Bargaining team membership, Bargaining unit scope, Board of trustees makeup
Cafeteria prices
Indemnity bonds
Management rights to union affairs
Past contract continuance
Retired employees' pension benefits
Strikebreaker employment, Supervisors included in the contract
Unfair labor charge settlements, Union dues, Union officer structure

Bargaining Types
Accommodating, Avoiding
Collaborating, Collective, Concessionary, Competing, Composite, Compromising
Distributive (zero-sum, win lose, hard)
Good faith
Integrative (nonzero-sum, win-win, soft)
Multi-employer (coordinated)
Productivity
Segmented, Surface

Employment-At-Will Major Exceptions
Good faith and fair dealing
Implied contract
Laws

Public policy

Impasses
Boycott
Economic strike
Grievance
Lawsuit, Lockout
Picketing
Sit down strike (illegal), Slowdown (illegal), Sympathy strike
Unfair labor practice strike
Wildcat strike (illegal)

Labor Relations Laws
Civil Service Reform, Clayton
Fair Labor Standards
Landrum-Griffin
Norris-LaGuardia
Postal Reorganization
Railway Labor
Sherman
Taft-Hartley
Wagner, Worker Adjustment and Retraining Notification

Union Security Clauses
Agency shop
Closed shop (illegal)
Dues checkoff
Maintenance of membership
Quasi union shop
Union shop

Section F Occupational Health, Safety, and Security

Criteria Used by OSHA to Go to Companies (in order)
Immediate danger
Catastrophe
Employee complaints
High hazard industries
Follow-up inspections

OSHA Violations
De Minimis
Repeat
Other-Than-Serious
Serious
Willful

Safety and Security Laws
Americans with Disabilities
Children's Online Privacy Protection, Computer Fraud and Abuse
Drug-Free Workplace
Electronic Communications Privacy
Gramm, Leach, Bliley
Federal Information Security Management
Health Information Portability and Accountability, Health Information Technology for Economic and Clinical Health, Homeland Security
Mine Safety and Health
Occupational Safety and Health
Sarbanes-Oxley
Unfair and Deceptive
U. S. Economic Espionage, USA Patriot, USA Patriot

Section G Miscellaneous

Human Resource-Related Certifications
Certified Benefits Professional, Certified Compensation Professional, Certified Executive Compensation Professional, Certified Professional in Learning and Performance, Certified Sales Compensation Professional
Global Professional in Human Resources, Global Remuneration Professional
Professional in Human Resources
Senior Professional in Human Resources

Human Resource-Related Organizations
American Society for Healthcare Human Resources Administration, American Society for Training and Development
College and University Professional Association for Human Resources
International Foundation of Employee Benefits Plans, International Public Management Association for Human Resources
Labor and Employment Relations Association

Society for Human Resource Management
WorldAtWork

Government Agencies Associated with HR
Bureau of Labor Statistics
Civil Service Commission
Department of Homeland Security, Department of Justice, Department of Labor
Equal Employment Opportunity Commission
Federal Emergency Management Agency, Federal Labor Relations Authority, Federal Mediation and Conciliation Service, Federal Service Impasses Panel
National Labor Relations Board, National Mediation Board
Occupational Safety and Health Administration, Occupational Safety and Health Review Commission, Office of Federal Contract Compliance Programs
Small Business Administration

Chapter Five

CREEDO Games

PURPOSE

Learn major human resource laws. CREEDO provides a consistent discussion of major human resource laws to help students study human resource management and prepare for various certification exams. CREEDO stands for the following:

Coverage—

Organizations: Which organizations are applicable to the law (private, public, size, contract value, other)

Individuals: What individuals are covered by the law?

Actions: What actions are covered by the law?

Regulations—

Restrictions: What restrictions are associated with the law?

Benefits: What benefits are associated with the law?

Enforcement—

Administration: Who will enforce the law?

Timing: What is the timing of the enforcement?

Penalties: What are the possible penalties?

Exceptions—

Organizations: Which organizations are specifically not covered by the law (private, public, size, contract value, other)?

Individuals: What individuals are specifically not covered by the law?

Actions: What actions are specifically not covered by the law?

Documents—

Records: What records are required by law and how long must such records be kept?

Posters: What posters are required by federal law?

Other—

Definitions: Explains select terms

Answers: Solutions to the fill-in-the-blank

WAYS TO PLAY

Fill in the Blank

One or More Players: The player who correctly fills in most of the blanks for each CREEDO game wins. Answers are at the bottom of each CREEDO table. The more answers you match, the higher you score. Players may either study the answers first and then play "Fill in the Blank" or start filling in the blanks without reading the answers first.

Dollar Bill Game

Version 1—Two or More Players: This game is originally a children's game in which one child memorizes all the details of the front of a dollar bill and the other child memorizes the details of the back for about three to five minutes. After that, one child asks detailed questions about the side the other child memorized. For example: Which direction is George Washington facing? Where is the Federal Reserve Bank located? Who is the Treasurer of the United States?

In a similar vein, one person can study one CREEDO law such as the Age Discrimination in Employment Act and the other person can study another CREEDO law such as the Child Labor Act. Take about ten minutes. Then, one person will ask detailed questions to the other about the law they memorized. Five minutes is just about right. For example, for the Age Discrimination Act, how big must a company be for it to apply? What are the restrictions? What are the benefits? How long must an HR record be kept?

Version 2—Two or More Players: Grab another HR book!! Have two or more people study different pages from the book for ten minutes and ask detailed questions for about five minutes.

Super Lecture

One or More Players: Grab one CREEDO law. Study it for five, ten, twenty, or more minutes—whatever is comfortable. Then give a lecture on it. If soloing, talk to an empty room or lecture to this book, spouse, cat, dog, brick, or cockroach—whoever or whatever is most attentive. If performing a group activity, lecturing to each other on a particular law can help everyone learn. After each lecture, ask questions about each law. Also, PowerPoint slides can be made.

Age Discrimination in Employment Act (ADEA)[1]

Provision	*Description*
Coverage	Organizations: Applies to employers with (1) ____ or more employees, including (2) _________, local and federal governments, employment agencies, and labor unions. Individuals: Protects individuals (3) _____ years of age or older from employment discrimination based on age. Protections apply to both (4) ___________ and job (5) ____________.
Regulations	Restrictions: Prohibits employers from using (6) ______ as a factor in making any decisions about workers, including hiring, pay, promotions, and layoffs. Programs cannot set age limits for trainees. Employers cannot take action against workers who file age discrimination charges. With some exceptions, employers cannot force employees to (7) _________ at a certain age.
Enforcement	Organization: The (8) __________________ enforces the ADEA. Timing: Employees must file with the Equal Employment Opportunity Commission within (9) __________days of the date discrimination is believed to have occurred. (10)________ have varying laws regarding time limits of filling claims. Penalties: Victims of age discrimination have several possible remedies: back pay, hiring, promotion, front pay, liquidated damages, and the payment of (11) _______ fees and related court costs.
Exceptions	Organization: Does not prohibit an employer from asking an applicant's age or (12) _________. Individuals: Does not apply to (13) __________ officials and (14) ___________ contractors. At an employer's request, an individual may agree to waive his or her rights under the ADEA. Actions: In some cases, age may be a (15) _____________ for the particular job.
Documents	Posters: The ADEA makes it unlawful to include age preferences and limits in job posters. A job notice or advertisement may specify an age limit where age is shown to be a (16) _______ necessity due to constraints on age concerning safety (airline pilots) and limits on hiring young workers due to the (17) _________ Act. Records: Employment records for payroll must be kept for (18) _____ years after the hiring. Applications may be kept for one year after hiring. If there are charges or

	lawsuits, records must be kept until they are over.
Other	Definitions: (19) ______________ (up to twice the amount of back pay) are what may be awarded in the event of a willful violation of the ADEA. An (20) ________________ is any person or entity regularly undertaking with or without compensation to procure employees for an employer. Answers: 1. twenty, 2. state, 3. forty, 4. employees, 5. applicants, 6. age, 7. retire, 8. Equal Employment Opportunity Commission (EEOC), 9. 300, 10. states, 11. attorney's, 12. date of birth, 13. elected, 14. independent, 15. Bona fide occupational qualification (BFOQ), 16. business, 17. Fair Labor Standards, 18. three, 19. Liquidated damages, 20. employment agency.

Child Labor Act[2]

Provision	Description
Coverage	Organizations: Applies to enterprises with employees engaging in (1) _________ commerce handling or producing goods for interstate commerce or goods that have been moved or produced for such commerce.
Regulations	Restrictions: Minors age (2) ___ and (3) _____ may perform any job not declared hazardous by the Secretary of (4) _____. Youths age (5) _____ and (6) _____ may work outside school hours in various non-hazardous jobs, with restrictions on the number of (7) _____ worked per week. Benefits: The provisions were enacted to ensure the safety, health, and education opportunities of young workers.
Enforcement	Administration: The Department of (8) ________________ (9) ____________ division investigates and enforces the Child Labor Act. Timing: When a penalty is assessed, employers have the right to file an exception to the determination within (10) ______ days of the receipt of notice. Penalties: Willful violations may be prosecuted criminally and the violator fined up to (11) ______ dollars for each violation. A second conviction may result in (12) ____________.
Exceptions	Individuals: Youths of any age can be employed by their (13) ________________ in non-hazardous occupations, and in any occupation in (14) ____________ on a farm owned by a parent/guardian. Minors employed as actors, delivering (15) _________, or making wreaths from home are also exempt.
Documents	Records: Employers must record the dates of birth for all employees under the age of (16) ______, as well as their daily starting and quitting times, their daily and weekly hours of work, and their occupations.
Other	Definitions: A (17) ________ is anyone under the age of eighteen. (18) ________occupations include manufacturing or storing explosives, logging, mining, roofing, excavating, meat packing, and, in general, operating power-driven machines or tools. (19) ________________ is employment of a minor in an occupation in which he or she does not meet the minimum age requirements. The Child Labor Act is an amendment to the (20) ______________. Answers: 1. interstate, 2. 16, 3. 17, 4. labor, 5. 14, 6. 15,

	7. hours, 8. Labor's, 9. Wage and Hour, 10. 15, 11. 10,000, 12. imprisonment, 13. parents/guardian, 14. agriculture, 15. newspapers, 16. 19, 17. minor, 18. hazardous, 19. Oppressive Child Labor, 20. Fair Labor Standards Act of 1938 (FLSA).

Civil Rights Act of 1964[3]

Provision	*Description*
Coverage	Organizations: Applies to employers with (1) _____ or more persons working (2) _____ or more calendar weeks per year, and are involved in interstate commerce. Also applies to state and local governments, employment agencies, and labor organizations. Individuals: Applies to any person regardless of their race, color, religion, gender or (3) ________________. Actions: Involves all employment-related actions such as hiring firing, compensation, training, etc.
Regulations	Restrictions: Prohibits employers from unlawful (4) _________ against persons of any race, color, religion, gender or national origin. Provides (5) _________ protection of the laws to all individuals. Enforces the constitutional right to vote, provides injunctive relief against (6) _____________ in public accommodations, authorized the (7) ________ to institute suits to protect constitutional rights in public facilities and public education, to prevent discrimination in federally assisted programs and to establish the (8) _________________ Opportunity Commission (EEOC). Benefits: Reduces discrimination based on race color, religion, gender, and national origin.
Enforcement	Administration: The (9) ____________________ enforces Title (10) ______ with private employers. The (11) ____________________ enforces Title VII with state and local government employers. The Attorney General may call for a (12) _________ action by filing a (13) ___________ to the appropriate district court. Timing: Charges must be filed with the (14) ________ within (15) ______ days of the alleged discriminatory act, unless the complainant has first filed with the appropriate state agency, in which case the complainant has (16) ______ days from the date of the alleged act to file with the EEOC. Penalties: (17) ________ pay is the most common form of relief. Compensatory damages, punitive damages, front pay, and injunctive relief are possible.
Exceptions	Organizations: Does not apply to an employer with respect to the employment of (18) __________ outside any state, or to a (19) ____________ corporation, association, or society with respect to the employment of individuals of a

	particular religion.
Documents	Records: For the purposes of an investigation of a charge, the (20) _________ shall have authority to examine witnesses under oath and to require the production of (21) ________evidence to the charge. Applications may be kept for one year after hiring. If there are charges or lawsuits, records must be kept until the lawsuits are finished. Posters: Every employer covered by the non-discrimination and EEO laws is required to display the appropriate EEO poster.
Other	Definitions: (22)______________ are allowed for future loss, emotional distress, pain and suffering, inconvenience, mental anguish and loss of enjoyment of life. (23)_______________________________ is an agency of the Department of Justice that enforces Title VII of the Civil Rights Act of 1964 and other antidiscrimination laws. (24) ____________________ is the pay that compensates the victim for anticipated future losses due to discrimination. (25)_________________ is available when there is an intentional discriminatory employment practice. Relief may involve reinstatement. (26)__________ are limited to cases where the employer has engaged in intentional discrimination and has done so with malice or reckless indifference to the rights of an aggrieved individual. Answers: 1. 15, 2. 20, 3. national origin, 4. employment practices, 5. equal, 6. discrimination, 7. Attorney General, 8. Equal Employment, 9. EEOC, 10. VII, 11. Department of Justice, 12. civil, 13. Complaint, 14. EEOC, 15. 180, 16. 300, 17. Back, 18. aliens, 19. religious, 20. EEOC, 21. documentary, 22. Compensatory damages, 23. EEOC, 24. Front pay, 25. Injunctive relief, 26. Punitive damages.

Civil Rights Act of 1991[4]

Provision	*Description*
Coverage	Organizations: Unlike other federal laws that apply to employers with (1) _____ employees or more, the Civil Rights Act of 1991 applies to (2) ______ employers. Individuals: Gives all (3) ________citizens the same full and equal benefits of all laws and proceedings enjoyed by (4) ____________ citizens. Protects American citizens working in (5) _______ countries for American companies. Actions: Involves all employment-related actions such as hiring firing, compensation, training, etc.
Regulations	Restrictions: Provides for the right to a (6) _________ by jury on discrimination claims and the possibility of emotional distress damages, while limiting the amount a jury could award the plaintiff. Prohibits discrimination in (7) __________ relationships. Prohibits (8) _________ of employment tests. Shifts the (9) _________ of proof in (10) __________ impact cases. Benefits: Reduces discrimination based on race color, religion, gender, and national origin.
Enforcement	Administration: The (11) _________________________ is the enforcement agency. Timing: A charge must be filed within (12) _____ days of the date on which the unlawful employment practice was alleged to have occurred. Penalties: (13) __________ damages may be awarded for emotional distress, suffering, mental anguish, loss of enjoyment of life, and other losses. (14) _______ damages may be recovered if the employer acted with malice or reckless indifference for the law.
Exceptions	Individuals: Plaintiff must prove that the discrimination in question was (15) __________ and reckless. Burden of proof is shifted from the defendant to the plaintiff.
Documents	Records: Employers must document (16) ________ cases of any type of discrimination. Posters: Posters describing the right to equal opportunity employment (17) __________ be shown by all relevant employers.
Other	Definitions: (18) ____________ is a court remedy that requires parties to perform certain acts or specifically perform a contract. (19) _________________ are an amount intended to cover actual losses.

	(20) _______________ are awarded in order to punish the offender. (21) ____________ is the practice of adjusting scores on a standardized by using separate curves for different racial groups. (22) _____________ is any test, job criterion, educational statistic, or crime statistic in which minorities are rated more poorly that whites. Answers: 1. 15, 2. all, 3. non-white, 4. white, 5. foreign, 6. trial, 7. contractual, 8. race-norming, 9. burden, 10. disparate, 11. Equal Employment Opportunity Commission (EEOC), 12. 90, 13. Compensatory, 14. Punitive, 15. intentional, 16. all, 17. must, 18. Equitable relief, 19. Compensatory damages, 20. Punitive damages, 21. Race-norming, 22. Disparate impact.

Consolidated Omnibus Budget Reconciliation Act (COBRA)[5]

Provision	*Description*
Coverage	Organizations: Applies to (1) _______ sector employers and those sponsored by (2) _____ and local governments. Covers group (3) __________ maintained by employers with (4) _____ or more employees who work more than 50 percent of the typical business days in the previous calendar year. Individuals: Applies to qualified beneficiaries and their (5) _________ or dependents who have lost health coverage due to (6) ________ events. If the employee, their spouse and dependent children all elect COBRA coverage, they will have (7) _____ months of coverage. The spouse and dependents alone can be covered up to (8) ______ months.
Regulations	Restrictions: Employers or (9) _________ administrators must provide an initial general notice to individuals entitled to COBRA benefits as well as provide qualified beneficiaries notice of a qualifying event. COBRA does not apply to plans sponsored by the (10) _______ Government. Benefits: Provides workers and their families the right to (11) ________ health benefits provided by their group health plan for a limited period of time under certain circumstances.
Enforcement	Administration: The Department of (12) _______________ has jurisdiction over private-sector group health plans. The Department of (13) _________________ administers the continuation of public-sector health plans. Timing: When a (14) ________ event occurs employers much notify plan administrators within (15) ____ days. Upon the receipt of notice, plan administrators must provide an (16) ______ notice to the qualified beneficiaries of their rights to elect COBRA coverage within (17) ____ days of initial receipt by the plan administrator. Beneficiaries must notify plan administrators within (18) ____ days of a divorce, legal separation, or change of a child's status as a dependent. Qualifying events for (19) ________________________ include voluntary or involuntary termination of the covered employee's employment for any reason other than gross misconduct, reduction in the hours worked by the covered employee, entitlement to Medicare, divorce or legal separation of the covered employee, or death of the

	covered employee. Coverage may be continued in case of a disability. To qualify, the beneficiary must first obtain a Social Security Administration ruling that he or she became (20) _________ within the first 60 days of COBRA coverage. Second, the employee must send the plan a copy of the Social Security ruling letter within 60 days of receipt and before the 18 month period ends. Then, the whole family qualifies for additional eleven months of coverage. Up to150% of the premium cost can be charged. If a qualified beneficiary waives coverage during the election period, he or she may (21) _________ the waiver of coverage before the end of the election period. A beneficiary may then choose the coverage. The plan need only provide continuation coverage beginning on the date the waiver is revoked. A COBRA qualifying event may occur when an employer's obligation to maintain health benefits under (22) _________________ ends. Penalties: A nondeductible excise tax of (23) ___ dollars per day per each qualified beneficiary for whom there has been a violation applies. Penalties of up to (24) ___ dollars per family per day also apply, but are subject to an annual maximum.
Exceptions	Organizations: Does not apply to organizations with less than (25) ____ employees, organizations who do not have (26) _________ for employees, (27) _____-related organizations or health plans sponsored by the (28) _______ government. Individuals: Individuals are not covered if their employer no longer has a health plan, if their employer has a different health plan, if the employee did not elect COBRA continuation within (29)____ days of receipt of notice, or if the employee is currently using the (30)__________________________.
Documents	Records: The employer should keep detailed records of COBRA (31) ___________.
Other	Definitions: The (32) _____________ is the time frame within which each qualified beneficiary must choose whether or not to extend coverage. A (33) ________________ is an individual covered by a group health plan on the day before a qualifying event who is an employee, the employee's spouse, or dependent child. Agents, independent contractors, and directors who

	are in a group health plan also may be qualified. A (34)_____________ includes voluntary or involuntary termination of employment for reasons other than gross misconduct, reduction in the number of hours of employment, job transitions, death, divorce, or other life events. Answers: 1. private, 2. state, 3. health plans, 4. 20, 5. spouse, 6. qualifying, 7. 18, 8. 36, 9. health plan, 10. Federal, 11. extend, 12. Labor & Treasury, 13. Health & Human Services, 14. qualifying, 15. 30, 16. election, 17. 14, 18. 60, 19. Spouses and dependent children, 20. disabled, 21. revoke, 22. FMLA, 23. 100, 24. 200, 25. 20, 26. health plans, 27. church, 28. Federal, 29. 60, 30. FMLA, 31. notifications, 32. election period, 33. qualifying beneficiary, 34. qualifying event.

Consumer Credit Protection Act[6]

Provision	*Description*
Coverage	Organizations: Applies to any business that acts as a (1) _______ that is any organization that regularly extends credit in conjunction with the sale of goods, services, or (2) _______ property. A creditor is also any (3) __________ issuer where finance charges apply. Individuals: Applies when these four conditions are met: the credit is offered or extended to (4) ________, the offering or extension of credit is done (5) ________, the credit is subject to a (6) ________ charge or is payable by a written agreement in more than four installments, and the credit is primarily for (7) _______, family or household uses. Actions: Applies to all extensions of (8) _______ payments for consideration of a finance charge. Protects the consumer and governs the actions of the (9) __________ agency.
Regulations	Restrictions: Creditors must clearly state the finance charge, (10) _________ rate, and methods of calculating the (11) __________ terms to the consumer of credit services. Benefits: Assures a meaningful disclosure of (12) ___________ and protects the consumer against inaccurate and unfair credit billing and credit card services.
Enforcement	Administration: The (13) ____________________ enforces the Consumer Credit Protection Act. Penalties: Violations of this stature are punishable by a fine not to exceed (14) _______ dollars or a jail term not to exceed (15) _____ year.
Exceptions	Organizations: Does not apply to organizational, commercial, or (16) ___________ credit transactions. Individuals: Individuals with an annual income exceeding (17) ________ dollars a year, and assets in excess of (18) ________ dollars can be exempt from normal credit terms disclosure.
Documents	Records: The Board of Governors shall publish model (19) _____________ forms and clauses for common transactions to enhance compliance.
Other	Definitions: (20) ________ (shortened name) refers to the Board of Governors of the Federal Reserve system. (21)_________ is the right granted by a creditor to a debtor to defer payment of debt or to incur debt and defer

	its payment. (22) ________ is to whom credit is offered or extended to in a credit transaction. Answers: 1. creditor, 2. real, 3. card, 4. consumers, 5. regularly, 6. finance, 7. personal, 8. deferred, 9. lending, 10. percentage, 11. interest, 12. credit, 13. Federal Trade Commission (FTC), 14. five thousand, 15. one, 16. governmental, 17. $200,000, 18. $1,000,000, 19. disclosure, 20. Board, 21. Credit, 22. consumer.

Davis-Bacon Act of 1931 and Related Acts (DBRA)[7]

Provision	*Description*
Coverage	Organizations: Applies to all contracting or (1)____________ employers, regardless of the number of employees, awarded contracts for (2)___________ of public buildings or public (3)_____, within the (4)______________ including the District of Columbia, valued in excess of (5)__________, that are in any part financed by the Federal Government. Individuals: Applies to all wage classes of laborers or mechanics employed by the contracting employer, and performing (6) __________ work directly related to the applicable contract(s).
Regulations	Restrictions: Only applies to contracts within the (7) _____________________. Prohibits employers from paying employees less than (8)__________________ rates. Benefits: (9) _________ can realize significant payroll tax savings.
Enforcement	Administration: The (10) _____________ division of the U.S. Department of Labor oversees the administration of the Act. (11) ________________ are assigned to each contract to oversee and ensure the delivery of the terms of each contract. Penalties: Firms that violate the act will be listed and will not be eligible for contract for a minimum of (12) ______ year(s).
Exceptions	Organizations: Does not apply to contracts executed outside the geographic area of the United States. Actions: In the event of a national emergency, the (13) __________ may suspend the Act.
Documents	Records: Contractors must file a (14) ___________________ for the preceding week's payroll period. Records must be kept for at least (15) ________ years from the contract completion date. Posters: (16) ___________ announcement posters must be displayed prominently on the job site. A copy of (17) __________ wages must be available for employee review.
Other	Definitions: (18) ________________ shall be the wages paid to the majority of the mechanics or laborers employed under Federal contracts that qualify under the Davis-Bacon Act. (19)______________________ provides for the payment of minimum wage and fringe benefits to laborers and

	mechanics engaged in construction activities under federal contracts. Wage rates and fringe benefits are based on Secretary of Labor calculations. Answers: 1. subcontracting, 2. construction, 3. works, 4. United States, 5. $2,000, 6. any, 7. United States, 8. locally prevailing wages, 9. Employers, 10. Wage & Hour, 11. Contracting officers, 12. three, 13. President, 14. Certified Payroll Report, 15. three, 16. Davis-Bacon, 17. prevailing, 18. Wage determination amount, 19. Bona fide fringe benefits.

Deficit Reduction Act of 1984 (DEFRA)[8]

Provision	*Description*
Coverage	Organizations: Applies to tax-exempt (1) ______ benefit organizations, specifically Voluntary Employee's Beneficiary Associations (VEBAs) and Supplemental Unemployment Benefit Trusts (SUBs). Actions: Affects welfare benefit plan funding, employee coverage decisions, and notification requirements regarding (2) __________ qualifications.
Regulations	Restrictions: Limits deductions for contributions to a welfare benefit fund to the equivalent sum of qualified (3) _________ costs and additions to a qualified (4) ___________. If the welfare benefit organization's benefits are found to be (5) _____________, that organization cannot qualify for (6) ________.
Enforcement	Administration: The (7) _________________ enforces DEFRA. Timing: Organizations must file a Form 1024 in order to be considered for tax (8) ___________.
Exceptions	Organizations: Deduction limits do not apply to any welfare benefit fund which is part of a (9) ________________. Actions: Group term life insurance, medical benefits, benefits under qualified group legal services plans, and dependent card assistance are not subject to (10)_____________ standards.
Documents	Records: Requires states to get documented evidence of an applicant's or recipient's citizenship and identity to initially receive Medicaid.
Other	Definitions: (11) _____________ is any benefit other than a benefit related to a transfer of property, employer's contributions to an employee's trust or annuity plan, or compensation under a deferred- payment plan, or certain foreign deferred compensation plans. (12)_____________________________ provide for the payment of benefits such as life and health insurance or other benefits to association members or their dependents. (13)____________________ form part of a plan that provides for the payment of supplemental unemployment compensation benefits. (14)__________________________________ are paid to an employee because of his/her involuntary separation from the employer due to a reduction in force, plant closings, accident or sickness, or similar conditions.

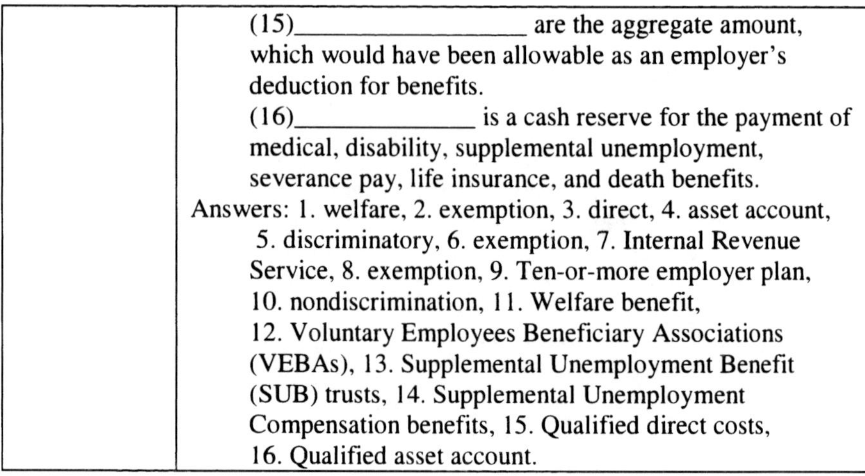

	(15)________________ are the aggregate amount, which would have been allowable as an employer's deduction for benefits. (16)_____________ is a cash reserve for the payment of medical, disability, supplemental unemployment, severance pay, life insurance, and death benefits. Answers: 1. welfare, 2. exemption, 3. direct, 4. asset account, 5. discriminatory, 6. exemption, 7. Internal Revenue Service, 8. exemption, 9. Ten-or-more employer plan, 10. nondiscrimination, 11. Welfare benefit, 12. Voluntary Employees Beneficiary Associations (VEBAs), 13. Supplemental Unemployment Benefit (SUB) trusts, 14. Supplemental Unemployment Compensation benefits, 15. Qualified direct costs, 16. Qualified asset account.

Employee Polygraph Protection Act of 1988 (EPPA)[9]

Provision	*Description*
Coverage	Organizations: Applies to all (1) _______ employers. Individuals: Applies to employees and prospective employees who seek employment through a (2) ___________ business are protected under this act. Actions: Covers (3) ________ testing of employees or potential employees by an employer or potential employer.
Regulations	Restrictions: The EPPA prohibits most private employers from using (4) _______ tests for pre-employment screening or during the course of employment. Employers are generally prohibited from requiring or (5) _________ an employee or potential employee to submit to a polygraph test. In addition, discharging, disciplining, or discriminating against an individual for (6) _______ to submit to a polygraph test is prohibited.
Enforcement	Administration: The (7) _____________ division of the Department of (8) _______________ administers and enforces this Act. Penalties: Violations are subject to a monetary penalty not to exceed (9) _______ dollars. Employer may also be liable for legal and equitable relief, including employment, (10) re-___________, promotion, payment of (11) __________ wages, and (12) ____________.
Exceptions	Organizations: Does not apply to (13) __________________ government agencies. Public school systems and correctional institutions also are exempt. Individuals: Does not apply to applicants to certain employers, such as (14) ________ service firms, and (15) ______________ manufacturers, distributors, and dispensers. Also, does not apply to employees that are (16) __________ suspected of involvement in theft or embezzlement that resulted in economic loss to the employer.
Documents	Records: Polygraph results are kept for (17) ______ years. The information obtained may be admissible in court. Posters: Every employer subject to the EPPA shall post a notice explaining the act in a prominent and (18) _________ place.
Other	Definitions: A (19) _________ test is an honesty test that involves a polygraph machine and a trained operator. Reasonable (20) ________ requires credible evidence but not certain evidence. Answers: 1. private, 2. commercial, 3. polygraph,

	4. polygraph, 5. requesting, 6. refusal, 7. Wage & Hour, 8. Labor, 9. $10,000, 10. instatement, 11. lost, 12. benefits, 13. Local, State, and Federal, 14. Security, 15. pharmaceutical, 16. reasonably, 17. three, 18. conspicuous, 19. polygraph, 20. suspicion.

Equal Pay Act of 1963 (EPA)[10]

Provision	*Description*
Coverage	Organizations: Applies to all (1) _______ organizations engaged in the production or manufacture of goods for (2) ________________. Individuals: Applies to all employees who are engaged in the production or manufacture of goods for commerce, and who are normally exempt according to the (3) ____________________. Benefits: Works to balance wages between men and women for (4) ___________ jobs.
Regulations	Restrictions: Prohibits employers from discriminating between employees on the basis of (5)_______ by paying wages to employees at a lower rate than other employees of the opposite gender in such establishment for equal (6)______, the performance of which requires equal skill, effort, (7)___________, and working (8)__________. The accused employer can avoid legal charges by providing one of the four legal defenses. These defenses permit uneven pay for equivalent work because of seniority, merit, quantity or quality of production, or any other condition besides gender.
Enforcement	Administration: The Equal Pay Act, part of the Fair Labor Standards Act (FLSA), is administered and enforced by the Equal Employment Opportunity Commission (EEOC). Timing: The statute of limitations is (9) _____ year(s) for normal violations or (10) _____ year(s) for willful violations. Penalties: Any employer in violation of the Equal Pay Act is subject to a fine not to exceed (11) ______ dollars with the possibility of imprisonment for second violations, and (12) ______ wages owed to the employee filing the suit.
Exceptions	Organizations: Does not apply to employers that do not have employees who are engaged in the production or manufacture of goods for commerce. Individuals: Pay exemptions are permitted when they are based on seniority, merit, quantity or quality of work, or a factor other than (13) _______. These are (14) ________ defenses and it is the employer's burden to prove their application. Any employee employed in a (15)_________ executive, administrative or professional capacity, any employee who is employed by a A (16)_________ organization operates less than seven

	months a year, and any employee in agriculture or seafood harvest that is hired for harvest labor and paid on a piece rate basis.
Documents	Records: Employers must preserve records which relate to the payment of wages, wage (17) _______, evaluations, job descriptions and any other relevant data on employees which explains the basis for payment of any wage. Records must be kept for at least (18) _______ year(s).
Other	Definitions: (19) ______________ are products that have been manufactured, produced, or generated by employees to be sold for profit by the employer. (20)________________ is a statute assigning a certain time after which rights cannot be enforced by legal action or offenses cannot be introduced to the courts. (21)________________ is a case which adequate evidence is available for a judgment to be reached, unless the evidence is challenged. (22)______________ is a government regulated and enforced lower limit on a value or pay amount. Answers: 1. employers, 2. commerce, 3. Fair Labor Standards Act, 4. comparable, 5. gender, 6. work, 7. responsibility, 8. conditions, 9. two, 10. three, 11. 10,000, 12. back, 13. gender, 14. affirmative, 15. bona fide, 16. non-profit, 17. rates, 18. two, 19. Goods for commerce, 20. Statute of limitations, 21. Prima facie case, 22. Price floor.

Fair Credit and Reporting Act of 1971 (FCR)[11]

Provision	*Description*
Coverage	Organizations: Covers consumer (1) ________ agencies that play a crucial role in the assembly and evaluation of consumers and consumer (2) ______. Covers any (3) ________, partnership, corporation, trust, estate, cooperative, association, government, or governmental subdivision, agency, or other entity.
Regulations	Restrictions: Consumer reporting agencies shall maintain (4) _______ procedures that require prospective users of credit information (5) ______ themselves, certify the (6) ______ for which the information is sought, and certify that the information will be used for no other purpose. The agencies shall make a reasonable (7) _____ to verify the identity of a new prospective user and the uses certified by a prospective user prior to (8) __________ a consumer report. Benefits: Controls access to consumers' credit and other personal information.
Enforcement	Administration: The (9) ___________________ is responsible for enforcement of the Act. Penalties: For intentional violations, persons shall be liable for a civil penalty of not more that (10) _____ per violation.
Exceptions	Organizations: Agencies or departments of the U.S. Government are exempt if the consumer report is relevant to a (11) ____________ investigation, if an investigation is within the (12) ___________ of the agency or department. Compliance may be affected if it results in endangering life or physical safety of any person, flight from prosecution, evidence tampering, compromise of classified information, or interference with the investigation of official proceedings.
Documents	Records: Whenever a consumer reporting agency prepares a consumer report, the agency shall follow reasonable procedures to insure (13) ________________ accuracy of the information concerning the individual about whom the report relates.
Other	Definitions: A (14)__________ is communication of any information by a consumer reporting agency concerning a consumer's credit worthiness, credit standing, credit capacity, character, general reputation, personal characteristics, or living mode that is used to help establish the consumer's eligibility for credit, insurance, or employment.

	A (15)____________________ is any person or entity that, for monetary fees or dues, regularly engages in assembling or evaluating consumer credit information to furnish consumer reports to third parties. Answers: 1. reporting, 2. credit, 3. individual, 4. reasonable, 5. identity, 6. purposes, 7. effort, 8. furnishing, 9. Federal Trade Commission (FTC), 10. $2,500, 11. national security, 12. jurisdiction, 13. maximum possible, 14. consumer report, 15. Consumer reporting agency.

Fair Labor Standards Act[12]

Provision	*Description*
Coverage	Organizations: Covers businesses whose annual gross volume of sales made or business done is not less than (1) __________ or is engaged in a hospital-related operation; a school for mentally or physically disabled; a preschool, an elementary or secondary school, or a higher education institution. Individuals: Applies to all employees of certain enterprises having workers engaged in or producing goods for interstate commerce or handling, selling, or working on goods or materials affected by the commerce.
Regulations	Restrictions: Covered (2) _______ employees must receive (3) _________ pay for hours worked over (4) _______ per workweek (any fixed and regularly recurring period of 168 hours — seven consecutive 24-hour periods) at a rate not less than one and one-half times the regular pay rate. There is no limit on the number of hours employees (5) ________ years or older may work in any workweek. The FLSA does not require overtime pay for work on weekends, holidays, or regular days of rest, unless overtime is worked on such days. The hours worked normally includes the time in which an employee is required to be on the employer's location. The act protects the education of minors and prohibits their employment in jobs and conditions that affect their health or well-being. Youths (6) _____ years or older may perform any job, whether hazardous or not, for unlimited hours; minors (7) ________ years old may perform any nonhazardous job for unlimited hours; and minors (8) _________ years old may work outside school hours in various nonmanufacturing, non-mining, nonhazardous jobs under the following conditions: no more than 3 hours on a school day, 18 hours in a school week, 8 hours on a non-school day, or 40 hours in a non-school week. Benefits: Covered, nonexempt workers are entitled to a minimum wage of (9) _________ per hour. Tipped employees are individuals engaged in occupations in which they customarily and regularly receive more than $30 a month in tips. The employer may consider tips as part of wages, but the employer must pay at least (10) ________ an hour in direct wages.

Enforcement	Administration: The Wage and Hour Division (WHD) of the U.S. (11) ______________________ (DOL) administers and enforces the FLSA concerning private sector organizations, state and local governments, and Federal employees of the Library of Congress, U.S. Postal Service, Postal Rate Commission, and the Tennessee Valley Authority. The FLSA is enforced by the U.S. Office of Personnel Management for employees of other Executive Branch agencies, and by the U.S. Congress for Legislative branch employees. Penalties: Willful violations may be criminally prosecuted. The violator can be fined up to (12) ________. A second conviction may result in imprisonment. Employers who violate the child labor provisions of the FLSA are subject to a civil money penalty of up to $11,000 for each violation.
Exceptions	Organizations: Exemptions from both minimum wage and overtime pay include executives and employees of certain seasonal amusement or recreational establishments, certain small newspapers, foreign vessels, fishing operations, newspaper delivery, and farm operations employing no more than 500 "person-days" of farm labor in any calendar quarter of the preceding calendar year. Casual babysitters and persons employed as companions to the elderly also are exemptions. Individuals: FLSA does not require vacations, holidays, severance, sick pay; meal periods, rest periods, holidays, vacations; premium pay for weekend or holiday work; pay raises, fringe benefits; discharge notices, reasons for discharge, or immediate payment of final wages to terminated employees.
Documents	Records: The FLSA requires employers to keep records on wages, hours, and other items. Posters: Employers must display an official (13) _______ outlining the requirements of the FLSA.
Other	Definitions: A (14) ________ is a period of 168 hours during 7 consecutive 24-hour periods. It may begin on any day of the week and at any hour of the day established by the employer. Two or more workweeks cannot be averaged. Employee coverage, compliance with wage payment requirements, and most exemptions are determined on a workweek basis. In general, (15) __________ includes time an employee must be on duty, on the employer's premises, or at any

	other designated workplace from the start to the end of the workday. Answers: 1. $500,000, 2. nonexempt, 3. overtime, 4. 40, 5. 16, 6. 18, 7. 16 and 17, 8. 14 and 15, 9. $7.25, 10. $2.13, 11. Department of Labor, 12. $10,000, 13. poster, 14. workweek, 15. hours worked.

Family and Medical Leave Act of 1993[13]

Provision	*Description*
Coverage	Organizations: Applies to Federal, state, and local government employees, and private-sector employers employing (1)____ or more employees within a 75 mile radius of the worksite, within (2)_______ or more workweeks in a calendar year. Individuals: Employees who have been employed for at least (3) ______ months, who have worked a minimum of (4) _______ hours during that period. State and U.S. government employees are covered by the Act.
Regulations	Restrictions: LEAVE: Employers must provide a maximum of (5) _______ weeks of unpaid leave to qualified employees because of medical reasons, child (6) ________, adoption, or foster care, care of a (7) ____________ member with a serious health condition. With serious health conditions, a child, spouse, or parent of the employee could qualify. Time associated for care of a child is covered in cases of child birth, adoption, and foster care. TIME: Leave taken under the FMLA for child birth or adoption is only permitted within 12 months of the birth child placement. Intermittent leave is permitted when medical leave reasons require it and the employer approves. There are up to 12 weeks of leave for qualifying events coming from a covered military member's active duty status and active duty notification. There are up to 26 weeks of leave in a single 12-month period to care for a covered service member who is seriously injured or ill due to active duty. Eligible employees are entitled to up to 26 weeks of all types of FMLA leave during a single 12-month period. NOTICE: If an employee is able to anticipate the need to take unpaid leave time under the FMLA, the individual must provide the employer with 30 day notice. RESTORATION: Upon returning to work, the employee must return to his or her previous position. In case the position is not available, the employer must furnish a

	position equivalent in pay and benefits. Benefits: The employer must maintain the same medical benefits for an employee who takes unpaid leave as with other employees.
Enforcement	Administration: The Act is enforced by the (8) ___________ division of the Department of (9) _____________. Timing: All claims must be made within (10) _____ year(s) of the alleged violation. Penalties: An employer in violation of the Act may be liable for (11) ______ equal to the amount of any wages, salary, benefits, or other compensation denied or lost by any employee.
Exceptions	Organizations: Public agencies, public elementary and secondary schools, and (12) __________ elementary and secondary schools are covered employers without regard to the number of employees employed.
Documents	Records: Records must be kept for (13) ______ year(s). The employer must maintain the following records: payroll information, notices of leave, dates and times leave was taken if less than one full work day, documentation regarding leave-related disputes, and employee benefits information. Posters: Posters must be posted by both employees and (14) __________. In workplaces where the majority of the employees do not speak English, the employer must provide notice in the language in which the employees are literate.
Other	Answers: 1. 50, 2. 20, 3. 12, 4. 1250, 5. 12, 6. birth, 7. family member, 8. Wage & Hour, 9. Labor, 10. two, 11. damages, 12. private, 13. three, 14. applicants.

Federal Insurance Contribution Act (FICA)[14]

Provision	*Description*
Coverage	Organizations: Involves companies that have at least one (1) ________. Individuals: An employee is covered by FICA if he or she performs services for an employer, is subject to the employer's (2) ____, or is a corporate director or officer. FICA generally applies to self-employed individuals, independent contractors, and partnership members. Other examples include drivers, insurance agents, home-workers, and traveling salespersons. Actions: All remuneration for employment, including the cash value or any non-cash remuneration, unless specifically (3) ________, is subject to FICA tax withholdings.
Regulations	Restrictions: Requires employers and employees to contribute 7.65% of the employees' earned wages each, for a total of 15.30% towards Social Security and (4) ________. Benefits: Upon disability or reaching retirement age (62 years), citizens are entitled to receive monetary benefits, funded by these taxes, in the form of (5) ____________ and/or Medicare.
Enforcement	Administration: The (6) ____________________ enforces FICA tax collections. The (7) ________________ disperses the funds. Penalties: Failure to keep records can result in a maximum prison sentence of (8) _____ year(s) and a maximum fine of (9)_________. An employee may sue an employer for failure to withhold FICA taxes.
Exceptions	Individuals: (10) ________ who are employed by a college or university, while enrolled and regularly attending its classes are not subject to FICA taxes. Also, Federal and (11) ______ employees, nonresident aliens, railroad workers, fishermen, public officials paid on a fee basis, work performed outside of the (12) ________, real estate agents, direct sellers, and newspaper carriers under the age of (13) ______ might not be subject to FICA taxes.
Documents	Records: Withheld FICA taxes are reported on IRS Form (14) _______. Employers are required to provide copies of IRS Form W-2 to the (15) ________________. Employers who pay too much in FICA taxes can request a refund of both the employee's and employer's shares of tax by filing IRS Form (16) ______.
Other	Definitions: (17) __________ taxable wage base is adjusted every year to reflect changes in average national wages.

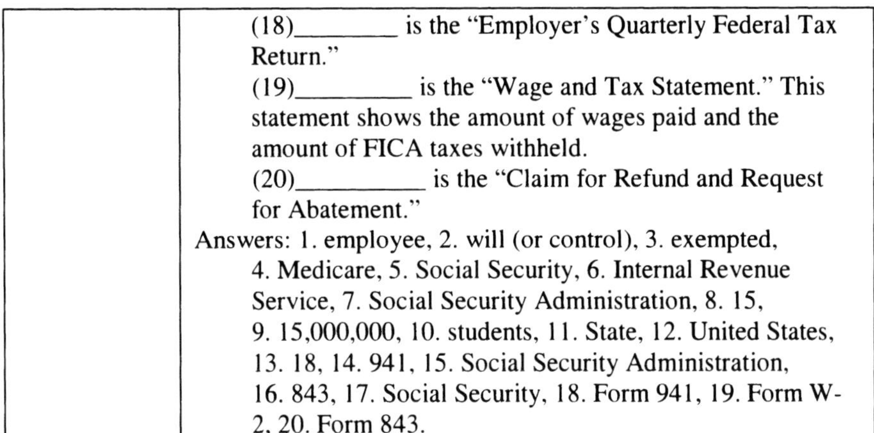

	(18)_______ is the "Employer's Quarterly Federal Tax Return." (19)________ is the "Wage and Tax Statement." This statement shows the amount of wages paid and the amount of FICA taxes withheld. (20)_________ is the "Claim for Refund and Request for Abatement." Answers: 1. employee, 2. will (or control), 3. exempted, 4. Medicare, 5. Social Security, 6. Internal Revenue Service, 7. Social Security Administration, 8. 15, 9. 15,000,000, 10. students, 11. State, 12. United States, 13. 18, 14. 941, 15. Social Security Administration, 16. 843, 17. Social Security, 18. Form 941, 19. Form W-2, 20. Form 843.

Federal Unemployment Tax Act (FUTA)[15]

Provision	*Description*
Coverage	Organizations: Applies to employers with (1) _____ or more employees within a twenty week time period or with a quarterly payroll of (2) ______ or more. Applies to employers engaged in intrastate, interstate, and (3) ________________ commerce. Individuals: Applies to employees working during any day of the week for (4) ______ weeks in a calendar year. Actions: Applies to any working activity by an employee for employer.
Regulations	Restrictions: The employer is required to pay a (5) _______ tax, into an unemployment fund, on the first (6) ______ paid to covered employees. Benefits: Employers receive assistance in finding new workers, and the unemployed receive financial help and job search assistance.
Enforcement	Administration: Enforced by the (7) ________________. Timing: Employees should file for unemployment immediately after losing employment. Benefits end upon hiring or after (8) _____ weeks. Penalties: Penalties for past due contributions are assessed at (9) __________rate of the tax due, or $10, whichever is greater.
Exceptions	Organizations: Government agencies and certain (10) __________ are not subject to the tax. Individuals: Employees working for non-covered employers.
Documents	Records: Employers are required to keep all records of employment taxes for (11) ____ year(s).
Other	Answers: 1. one, 2. $1,500, 3. foreign, 4. twenty, 5. payroll, 6. $7,000, 7. Internal Revenue Service, 8. 26, 9. 2%, 10. non-profits, 11. four.

Health Insurance Portability and Accountability Act of 1996[16]

Provision	*Description*
Coverage	Organizations: Applies to any employer's group health plan or group health insurance plan which has, at the beginning of the year, (1) ______ or more current employees enrolled in the plan. Individuals: Applies to individuals with group health care plans, that are starting a new job, or (2) ________ jobs.
Regulations	Restrictions: Limits the use of (3) _________ health condition exclusions. Prohibits group health plan providers from (4) _________________ against employees, or employee's dependents, with past or present poor health, by denying coverage or requiring additional fees for coverage. Benefits: Guarantees availability and (5) ___________ of coverage for employers in the group market.
Enforcement	Administration: Enforced by the (6) ___________________________. Privacy issues within the Act are enforced by the Department of (7) _______________. Timing: Violations must be corrected within (8) ____ day(s). To be covered by the Act, individuals cannot let their coverage lapse for more than (9) ____ day(s). Complaints must be filed within (10) _____day(s). Penalties: A fine of (11) ______ per day for each affected employee is applicable. Total fines per provider, for violations of identical requirements or prohibitions, cannot exceed (12) _______ per calendar year.
Exceptions	Individuals: The Act does not control the amount an insurer may charge for coverage, or permit individuals to keep previous health coverage providers when moving to a new job.
Documents	Records: Group health plans and health insurance issuers are required to furnish a (13) ____________________ to an individual to provide documentation of the individual's prior creditable (14) ________.
Other	Definitions: (15) _____________ health conditions are past or present physical or mental conditions for which medical, diagnosis or care was recommended or received. Answers: 1. 2, 2. switching, 3. pre-existing, 4. discriminating, 5. renewability, 6. Center for Medicare & Medicare Services, 7. Health and Human Services, 8. 30, 9. 63, 10. 180, 11. $100, 12. $25,000, 13. Certificate of Coverage, 14. coverage, 15. Pre-existing.

Health Maintenance Organization Act of 1973[17]

Provision	*Description*
Coverage	Organizations: Applies to any employer with (1) ______ or more employees, pays the (2) ___________, and which offers a qualified Health Maintenance Organization (HMO) as an insurance option for its employees. Actions: Allows individuals, who have another health plan with (3) _________ or better coverage, the option to use another plan if proof of equality is provided.
Regulations	Restrictions: Employers offering a federally qualified HMO option must offer the HMO so that no other insurance option is favored over the HMO. Employers that (4) _______ to any other insurance options, must also contribute to the HMO's monthly premium to eliminate financial (5) ___________ against the employees enrolled in the HMO. Benefits: Eliminates regulatory barriers which hinder HMO development which may reduce costs.
Enforcement	Administration: The Department of (6) _______________ is the regulatory body which enforces the Act. Penalties: Employers found in violation of the act are subject to a civil penalty not to exceed (7) ________. Employers with repeated violations may be subject to Civil Action.
Exceptions	Individuals: Employees living (8) _______ of the area in which the HMO is offered, may be exempt.
Documents	Records: Availability of an HMO, the name and address of the available HMO and other pertinent information must be available through the employer's health programs description.
Other	Definitions: An (9) ________ is health care coverage provided by hospitals, doctors, and other providers with which it has a contract. Hospitals receive more patients while offering their services at a discount. This allows the HMO to charge a lower monthly premium. Answers: 1. 25, 2. equal, 3. minimum wage, 4. contribute, 5. discrimination, 6. Health and Human Services, 7. $10,000, 8. outside, 9. HMO.

Immigration Reform and Control Act of 1986 (IRCA)[18]

Provision	*Description*
Coverage	Organizations: All employers, public and (1) _______, including governmental entities, are covered by this Act. Individuals: The Act requires that all U.S. residents, including (2) ________, who are hired to work within the United States, must provide documentation for proof of (3) ________ and work authorization. Actions: Applies to employer activities such as; hiring, discharging, recruiting, or referring on a fee basis.
Regulations	Restrictions: Prohibits employers from knowingly hiring an (4) ____________ alien, from continuing to employ an unauthorized alien, and penalizes any failure to provide the (5) ______________ form. Benefits: Prohibits employment discrimination based on (6)____________ or citizenship
Enforcement	Administration: The (7) ___________________, has jurisdiction over and enforces the IRCA. The (8) ______________ has jurisdiction over the anti-discrimination portion of the Act. Timing: Employers must complete and submit the (9) ___________________ Verification Form (I-9 Form) within (10) _____ day(s) or hiring an individual. Penalties: Hiring violations may result in up to (11) _______ in fines and/or six months in prison. Record keeping violations may result in fines not to exceed $1000.
Exceptions	Organizations: Employers do not have to provide the I-9 form for employees hired before 11-8-1986 who left employment or were recruited or referred for a fee before 6-1-1987. Individuals: I-9 Forms do not have to be provided for (12) ____-employed persons, independent contractors, or private home domestic employees working on an intermittent or sporadic basis.
Documents	Records: Employers are required to keep I-9 forms for each new employee for (13) ___ year(s), or one year after the employee's last day, whichever is longer.
Other	Definitions: A (14) _______ is a native or naturalized person who owes allegiance to a government. An (15) ________________ is not a U.S. citizen, and does not possess the required documentation for proof of identity or work authorization as required by the IRCA. Answers: 1. private, 2. citizens, 3. identity, 4. unauthorized, 5. I-9, 6. National origin, 7. Immigration and

	Naturalization Service, 8. Department of Justice, 9. Employment eligibility, 10. three, 11. $10,000, 12. Self, 13. three, 14. citizen, 15. unauthorized alien.

Landrum-Griffin Act/ Labor-Management Reporting and Disclosure Act (LMDRA)[19]

Provision	*Description*
Coverage	Organizations: Applies to labor (1) ______ that are covered by the National Labor Relations Act (NLRA), as well as railroad and airline workers. It also covers unions representing U.S. Postal Service. Individuals: Covers (2) _____ within the unions under the NLRA, railroads, and airlines. Does not cover unions where the employees are strictly of state and local government. Actions: Union officials and (3) _______ must be elected democratically. Establishes a (4) ____________ for union workers.
Regulations	Restrictions: The Act requires the reporting and disclosure of certain (5) __________ transactions and (6) ___________ practices of labor organizations and employers. Benefits: Promotes democratic procedures by establishing a (7) __________ for union members, reporting requirements for labor organizations, standards for election of union officers, safeguards for protecting funds and assets. Gave union members (8) _____ rights within their organization. Local unions and international unions elect officers through (9) __________. International unions must hold elections at least every 5 years, intermediate bodies every 4 years, and local unions every 3 years. A parent union can place a smaller body under trusteeship. Trusteeships must comply with the (10) _______ and the constitution and bylaws of the labor organization.
Enforcement	Administration: The Secretary of Labor enforces many provisions and has delegated that authority to the Office of Labor-Management Standards of the Department of Labor's (11) _________________ Administration. Penalties: Most violations are penalized on a case by case basis. Embezzlement of union funds can result with a maximum of (12) _______ in fines and/or (13) ____ years in prison. Persons convicted of these crimes may not hold union office or employment for up to 13 years after the conviction or the end of imprisonment.
Exceptions	Individuals: Former members of the (14) ________ party and convicted felons are prohibited from holding a union (15) _____ for 5 years after party membership resignation

	or release from prison.
Documents	Records: Every labor organization must adopt a (16) __________ and bylaws and file a copy with the Secretary of Labor. Unions must also submit annual (17) _________ reports to the Department of Labor. The LMRDA requires that unions keep records of their financial operations and election information for at least five years.
Other	Definitions: (18) ___________ are organizations of workers formed for the purpose of advancing its members' interests with respect to wages, benefits, and working conditions. Answers: 1. unions, 2. members, 3. officers, 4. democracy, 5. financial, 6. administrative, 7. Bill of Rights, 8. voting, 9. secret ballot, 10. LMRDA, 11. employment standards, 12. 250,000, 13. 5 years, 14. labor, 15. office, 16. constitution, 17. financial, 18. unions.

Mental Health Parity Act of 1996 (MHPA)[20]

Provision	*Description*
Coverage	Organizations: Applies to public employers with at least (1) ______ employees who provide mental health (2) ________ coverage; with fully insured state-regulated health plans and (3) ________ plans that are exempt from state laws under the Employee Retirement Income Security Act (ERISA). Individuals: Applies to employees and their dependents who are suffering from a (4) _____ disorder, mental impairment, severe mental impairment, or (5) __________ disorder which is of the severity to require (6) _____ treatment.
Regulations	Restrictions: Prohibits employers, and group health care insurers, and Health Maintenance Organizations from setting annual or (7) _____ dollar limits on mental health benefits that are lower than the limits set on medical and surgical benefits. (8) ______ must retain discretion of the extent and scope of mental health benefits offered to employees and their families such as cost sharing information and days of coverage.
Enforcement	Administration: The act has the concurrent jurisdiction of the Department of Labor, Department of the Treasury, and (9) ________________. The Secretary of Labor and Health and Human Services actively participates in random audits of health plans and make sure these audits are conducted to ensure that (10) ______ are in compliance with this Act.
Exceptions	Individuals: Those suffering from substance abuse or (11) _______ dependencies are not considered mentally ill. Actions: Does not require mental health (12) _______ to be offered in health insurance plans. Coverage in connection with Medicare and (13) _______ are not included. Does not apply to small group health plans or health insurance coverage in the individual market. If large group health plans can demonstrate that compliance to MHPA will (14) _____ their cost by at least one percent, then it does not need to apply to coverage. This exemption is based on at least (15) _____ months of claims and not an increase in insurance premiums.
Documents	Records: All (16) ________ records are to be kept confidential.
Other	Definitions: (17) _________________ refers to benefits with

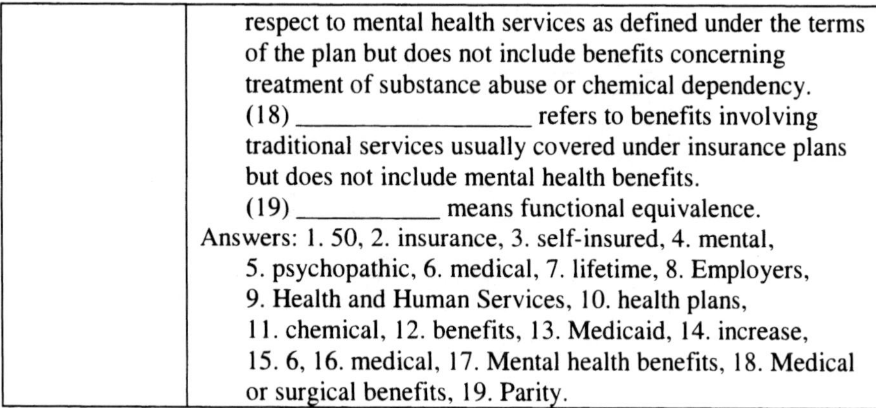

	respect to mental health services as defined under the terms of the plan but does not include benefits concerning treatment of substance abuse or chemical dependency. (18) ________________ refers to benefits involving traditional services usually covered under insurance plans but does not include mental health benefits. (19) __________ means functional equivalence. Answers: 1. 50, 2. insurance, 3. self-insured, 4. mental, 5. psychopathic, 6. medical, 7. lifetime, 8. Employers, 9. Health and Human Services, 10. health plans, 11. chemical, 12. benefits, 13. Medicaid, 14. increase, 15. 6, 16. medical, 17. Mental health benefits, 18. Medical or surgical benefits, 19. Parity.

Military Selective Service Act of 1967[21]

Provision	*Description*
Coverage	Individuals: All male U.S. citizens, and certain non-citizens, between the ages of (1) _____ and (2) _____ are required to register for selective service unless they are deferred or (3) _______. (4)____________ objector status may be granted to member of certain religious organizations.
Regulations	Restrictions: Conscientious objectors may be required to perform alternative (5) ___________.
Enforcement	Administration: The (6) ______________________ is the agency that registers individuals and chooses individuals should the draft be reinstated. Timing: Individuals have (7) _____ day(s) after their eighteenth birthday to register. Registered individuals, under the age of 26 have 10 days to provide a change of address to the Selective Service System. Penalties: Individuals failing to register before their 26th birthday may be subject to fines not to exceed (8) ________ and/or up to (9) _______ year(s) in prison. Individuals that fail to register may be denied federal financial aid and may not be employed by the federal government.
Exceptions	Individuals: Individuals do not have to register if they are currently enlisted, mentally or physically disabled, or female. A few other exceptions apply.
Documents	Records: After registration, individuals receive a (10) ______________ acknowledgement form with a registration number.
Other	Definitions: A (11) _________________ refuses to serve in the armed forces or bear arms on moral or religious grounds. A (12) ________ of service is the official postponement of military service. An (13) ________ of service is the permanent preclusion from military service. Answers: 1. 18, 2. 26, 3. exempt, 4. conscientious, 5. service, 6. Selective Service System, 7. 30, 8. $250,000, 9. five, 10. registration, 11. conscientious objector, 12. Deferment, 13. Exemption.

Norris-LaGuardia Act of 1932/ Anti-Injunction Act[22]

Provision	*Description*
Coverage	Organizations: Provides (1) ___________ the right to organize, (2) ______, boycott, and other legal strategies against management without Federal Court interference. Individuals: Provides (3) _________ with the right to participate in labor unions.
Regulations	Restrictions: Curtails intervention by Federal Courts by limiting their ability to issue (4) __________ orders and (5) ___________ against peaceful striking, assembling, patrolling, or publicizing facts about the labor dispute. Outlaws the use of (6) __________ contracts (pledges by workers not to join a union) by employers. Exempts labor unions from (7) _________ laws. The act broadly defines labor disputes. No restraining order or (8) _______ relief will be granted to anyone who has not complied with the law. Benefits: Allows unionized and non-unionized employees to engage in union activities without reprisal fears.
Enforcement	Administration: The (9) ____________________ oversees Act enforcement. Federal courts can only intervene if illegal activities are committed or threatened, or if great harm will come if there is no injunction. Timing: Temporary injunctions without notice are only valid for (10) _____ day(s). Penalties: Unions are immune from (11) ______ suits. Federal courts must have strict procedures to protect any person affected in a dispute that involves an injunction or when harm to person or property is threatened.
Exceptions	Individuals: No individual officers, (12) _______, or agents shall be held responsible or liable in any court for unlawful acts of labor unions in a labor dispute except when clear proof of (13) ____________ in or authorization of said unlawful act is provided. Actions: Cases involving (14) ___________ strikes are not immune to injunction.
Documents	None

Other	Definitions: A (15) __________ is an organization of wage earners who advance their concerns with wages, benefits, and working conditions. An (16) _________ is a court order prohibiting a party from a specific course of action such as going on strike. A (17) ________________ is an employer-employee contract where employment is conditional on non-involvement with union activities. (18)______________ are federal and state statutes designed to promote and remove restrictions on interstate commerce. A (19) _____________ is a strike undertaken by workers without approval from union officials. Answers: 1. Labor unions, 2. strike, 3. employees, 4. restraining, 5. injunctions, 6. yellow-dog, 7. anti-trust, 8. Injunctive, 9. National Labor Relations Board (NLRB), 10. 5, 11. damage, 12. members, 13. participation, 14. wildcat, 15. labor union, 16. injunction, 17. yellow-dog, 18. anti-trust laws, 19. wildcat strike.

Occupational Safety and Health Act of 1970 (OSHA)[23]

Provision	*Description*
Coverage	Organizations: Applies to all (1) ________ operating within the United States, excluding federal, state, and local government employees. (2) ________ groups apply if they employ workers for secular reasons. Individuals: Applies to every (3) _________ working for a covered employer. Actions: Created a National Advisory Committee and the (4) ____________________________ that create and enforce the standards.
Regulations	Restrictions: Requires every covered employer to furnish each of their employees' employment, and a place of employment, which are free from recognized (5) __________ that are causing or are likely to cause death or serious physical (6) _____________. (7)_________ must comply with all rules and regulations that apply to their own actions and conduct. Major regulations include; access to medical and (8) ________ records, availability of personal protective (9) __________, and hazard (10) ____________. Benefits: Provides regulations for (11) _____________ and healthy working environments by enforcing safe standards and conditions . It also provides research, information, education, and training.
Enforcement	Administration: The Act is enforced by the Secretary of the Department of (12) _______________ and OSHA. Every establishment covered by the Act is subject to inspection by OSHA (13) ______________________ (CSHOs). OSHA (14) ______ may enter to inspect and investigate areas covered under this Act during regular working hours without much advance warning. Timing: If safety (15) ________ have been found by inspectors, a timeframe will be established to correct the violation. Employers must report the work-related death of an employee within 8 hours to OSHA. Penalties: There are four types of citations with fines ranging from $1000 to (16) _______, and imprisonment of six months to (17) ___ year(s), depending on the severity of the violation. The four types are; serious, other than serious, (18) _______ and willful.
Exceptions	Organizations: The Act does not have jurisdiction over any federal, state, or local employees, unless they have

	established an (19) __________. It also does not include self-employed and family farms.
Documents	Records: Employers with (20) _____ or more employees must record all work-related injuries and illnesses with OSHA Form (21) ______. Posters: Applicable (22) _______ Sheets and OSHA's (23) __________________________ poster must be conspicuously posted.
Other	Definitions: (24) ____________________ sheets are information regarding the use, effects, treatment for overexposure to hazardous chemicals or materials. (25)__________________ are standards that require certain methods, or the adoption or use of certain practices necessary to provide safe employment. (26)________________ is specialized clothing, garment, or equipment worn by employees for the protection or promotion against health and safety hazards. A (27) ____________ is a clause that states every working man and woman must be provided with a safe and healthy work environment. Answers: 1. employers, 2. employees, 3. religious, 4. Occupational Safety and Health Administration, 5. hazards, 6. harm, 7. employees, 8. exposure, 9. equipment, 10. communication, 11. safe, 12. Health and Human Services, 13. Compliance Safety and Health Officers, 14. inspectors, 15. violations, 16. $20,000, 17. 1, 18. repeat, 19. OSHA plan, 20. 11, 21. 300A, 22. Material Safety Data, 23. Safe and Healthful Workplace, 24. Material Safety Data, 25. Occupational and health standards, 26. Personal protective equipment, 27. General Duty Clause.

Patient Protection and Affordable Care Act (PPACA)[24]

Provision	*Description*
Coverage	Organizations: Applies to employers with more than (1) _____ employees. They must automatically enroll new full-time employees in coverage. Any employer with more than (2) _____ full-time employees that does not offer coverage and has at least one full-time employee receiving premium assistance tax credit will make a payment of (3) ________ per full-time employee. Individuals: To provide health care coverage for more than (4) _____ percent of Americans. Actions: Requires all insurance companies to cover all applicants with a new minimum standards regardless of gender and (5) _____________.
Regulations	Restrictions: Eliminates lifetime and unreasonable annual limits on health benefits. Cap insurance company non-medical, (6) __________ expenditures. Insurers are prohibited from denying coverage or setting rates based on health status, medical condition, claims experience, genetic information, or evidence of domestic violence. Benefits: Extends dependent coverage up to age (7) _____. Require coverage and provide funding of preventative services and immunizations. Develop uniform coverage documents. Establish (8) __________ to provide health insurance options online. Create effective appeals process for health insurance coverage. Provide refundable tax credits for Americans at different income levels. Enhance healthcare workforce education.
Enforcement	Administration: The Secretary of (9) ____________ (HHS) will establish a national public option (Community Health Insurance Option) and permit states to opt-out with their own (10) __________. Timing: The individual mandate requires that all eligible Americans have at least basic health coverage by (11) _____. Penalties: Most individuals will be required to maintain minimum essential health coverage or pay a penalty of $95 in 2014, $350 in 2015, $750 in 2016, and indexed afterward. For individuals under 18, the penalty is (12) ______the amount of adults.
Exceptions	Individuals: Does not apply to religious (13) ____________, those who cannot afford coverage, taxpayers with incomes less than 100 percent (14) _______________(FPL), Indian tribe members, those

	who receive a hardship waiver, individuals not lawfully present, jailed individuals, and those not covered for less than three (15) _______.
Documents	Records: Requires employers to report the cost of coverage under an employer-sponsored group health plan on an employee's Form (16) ______, Wage and Tax Statement. Individuals must either have health coverage for each month, qualify for an (17) ___________, or make a payment when filing their (18) ___________ income tax return.
Other	Definition: The Federal Poverty Line (FPL) is about $88,000 for a family of four. Answers 1. 200, 2. 50, 3. $750, 4. 94, 5. pre-existing, 6. administrative, 7. 26, 8. Internet portal, 9. Health and Human Services, 10. Exchanges, 11. January 31, 2014, 12. half, 13. objectors, 14. Federal Poverty Line, 15. months, 16. W-2, 17. exemption, 18. federal.

Postal Reorganization Act of 1970 (PRA)[25]

Provision	*Description*
Coverage	Organizations: Applies to the United States Postal Service (USPS) and all post offices; urban and (1) _________. Individuals: Applies to all Postal Service (2) __________ and users.
Regulations	Restrictions: Establishes the USPS as a (3) ________ wholly-owned by the government. Eliminates the Postmaster General as a (4) ________- level position. Allows the terms and conditions of employment to be decided through (5) ____________________. Prohibits closure of offices operating at a (6) _______. Established a Board of (7) _______ to oversee the USPS. Requires that the postal service get prior approval from the (8) ______________ before they offer a new service, change existing services or increase or decrease rates. Benefits: A labor contract is achieved through collective bargaining. Congress (9) _______________ the Postal Service with the PRA. They effectively removed direct governmental control from the calculation of (10) ______, hours, and benefits for non- management employees. Employment terms are determined through a collective bargaining that can include (11) ________, fact finding, and arbitration. Postal workers do not have the right to (12) __________. Wage scales are determined through (13) _________ comparability with the private sector.
Enforcement	Administration: The (14) ________________ controls all expenditures of the Postal Service, sets all policies, and appoints the Postmaster General. The (15) __________ Commission recommends postal rates. The (16) ____________________ oversees the collective bargaining of employees.
Documents	Records: Every year, the USPS must submit a (17) ______ for its operating expenses to the President.
Other	Answers: 1. rural, 2. employees, 3. corporation, 4. cabinet, 5. collective bargaining, 6. deficit, 7. Governors, 8. Postal Rate Commission, 9. deregulated, 10. wages, 11. mediation, 12. strike, 13. pay, 14. Board of Governors, 15. postal rate, 16. National Labor Relations Board, 17. budget.

Pregnancy Discrimination Act of 1978 (PDA)[26]

Provision	*Description*
Coverage	Organizations: Applies to all employers including; (1) ______, state, and local governments, employment agencies, and labor organizations. Individuals: Applies to women who are (2) ______ or affected by other related conditions must receive the same treatment as other (3) _________ or employees with similar work abilities.
Regulations	Restrictions: (4) __________ on the basis of pregnancy, childbirth, or related medical conditions constitutes unlawful sex discrimination under (5) ________. Pregnancy related benefits cannot be limited to (6) ______ employees. Pregnant employees must be permitted to work as long as they are able to (7) _____ their jobs. Employers cannot refuse to hire a pregnant applicant solely because she is pregnant. Employers cannot prohibit an employee from returning to work for a (8) ___________ length of time after childbirth. Employees with pregnancy-related disabilities must be treated the same as other (9) ______________ disabled employees. Benefits: Any health insurance the employer provides must cover pregnancy similarly to other medical conditions. Employers must hold a job open for a pregnancy-related (10) ______________ the same length of time jobs are held open for employees on sick or disability leave.
Enforcement	Administration: This Act is enforced by the (11) _____________________________. Individuals who feel that they have been discriminated against under this act have (12) ___ day(s) after the incident to report the violation. Employers cannot (13) _______ against an individual for opposing employment practices that discriminate based on pregnancy, filing a discrimination charge, or being involved with an investigation law suit.. Penalties: Employees and applicants that have been discriminated against under this act may be entitled to remedies such as reinstatement or back pay, damages, and compensations. The employer may also be subject to (14) ______ damages.
Exceptions	Organizations: All employers with (15) ____ or more employees are subject to PDA. Under Title VII and FMLA, state and local government employers are

	mandated no matter the number of employees. (16) ______________ that is required under this act does not have to cover abortions except where the life of the mother is in danger. Employers also must provide equal level of health insurance both to male and female employees.
Documents	Posters: Posters outline employees' rights and are required to be conspicuously posted.
Other	Definitions: (17) ___________ disabled employees have a physical or mental disability that can reasonably be expected to resolve itself. (18)_________ of the Civil Rights Act prohibits employment discrimination based on race, color, religion, sex, and national origin. Answers: 1. federal, 2. pregnant, 3. applicants, 4. Discrimination, 5. Title VII, 6. married, 7. perform, 8. predetermined, 9. temporarily, 10. absence, 11. Equal Employment Opportunity Commission, 12. 180, 13. retaliate, 14. punitive, 15. 15, 16. Health insurance, 17. Temporarily, 18. Title VII.

Privacy Act of 1974[27]

Provision	*Description*
Coverage	Organizations: Applies to all governmental (1) ________ and specific federal contractors who operate Privacy Act systems of records for federal agencies. Individuals: Covers all individuals who are (2) ________ of the U.S., or aliens admitted for permanent residency, and (3) ______ or legal guardians of minors or (4) ________ persons. Covers all people who have attended a school of (5) ____________ and continues to cover them until they are deceased. Actions: Applies to the sharing of (6) ___________ held by governmental agencies, including health information.
Regulations	Restrictions: Requires written (7) ______ of individuals in order for any recipient agency to disclose their records to any other source. An individual's name or (8) _______ may not be sold or rented by any agency unless they are otherwise permitted to be made (9) ____________. Recipient agencies must follow (10) ____________ pertaining to the collection and use of (11) ____________. A person cannot be required by any government agency (federal, state, or local) to give their (12) ____________ to receive any type of right or benefit unless required by Congress. Benefits: Protects certain federal records pertaining to individuals, and prohibits (13) ___________ disclosures of said records by limiting matching programs. Gives individuals the right to access and (14) _____ their private records. U.S. citizens and permanent residents have the right to sue the government if their (15) ________ under the privacy act have been violated.
Enforcement	Administration: Enforced by Federal and (16) ______ courts. Timing: Individuals have (17) ______ days after the date of acknowledgement of a request to amend, to amend their records. Requests to review records must be honored within (18) _____ days of the request. Penalties: Willful disclosure of information is a misdemeanor with a maximum fine (19) ______. If an agency refuses to (20) ______ an individual's records when requested, the individual has the right to sue in civil court to have the record amended and have dispute-related costs reimbursed.
Exceptions	Individuals: Does not cover non-citizens or illegal aliens. Act does not apply to any disclosure that is being used in a

	system of records that existed before January 1, 1975. Actions: The act does not cover records such as credit reports, (21) _______ statements, or medical records. The act does not apply during criminal investigations.
Documents	Records: Each agency shall prepare and make (22) _______ an index of all major information systems of the agency and a handbook showing how to obtain agency public information. Timing: Agency records about disclosure must be kept for (23) ____ years or the lifetime of the record, whichever is longer.
Other	Definitions: A (24) _______________ includes any agency or contractor thereof receiving records contained in a system of records from a source agency. A (25) ____________ is a group of records under the control of an agency from which information can be retrieved by using an identifier associated with an individual such as name and Social Security number. Answers: 1. agencies, 2. citizens, 3. parents, 4. disabled, 5. higher education, 6. private records, 7. consent, 8. address, 9. public, 10. "fair information practices," 11. personal information, 12. Social Security number, 13. unauthorized, 14. amend, 15. rights, 16. state, 17. 10, 18. 30, 19. $5,000, 20. amend, 21. bank, 22. public, 23. five, 24. recipient agency, 25. system of records.

Racketeer Influenced and Corrupt Organizations Act (RICO)[28]

Provision	*Description*
Coverage	Organizations: Applies to any (1) _________ or group of individuals whom engage in a pattern of (2) ___________ activities. Individuals: Applies to any individual employed by or associated with a covered enterprise or group. Actions: Applies to racketeering activities must be in a pattern of (3) __________, continuity, or having multiple schemes.
Regulations	Restrictions: It is unlawful for a person or persons through the use of an enterprise a pattern of racketeering activity to: (4) ______ money, to acquire or maintain an interest in said enterprise, to benefit from (5) ___________ activity, or to (6) _______ to engage in any of the aforementioned activities.
Enforcement	Administration: The act is enforced by (7) _____________ courts. Timing: The defendant cannot be prosecuted unless he/she has committed (8) ________ predicate act, forming a pattern, within (9) _____ years or less of the indictment. Once a victim is aware of their injury they have (10) _____ years to bring it to claim. Penalties: Plaintiffs may be awarded (11) _______ amount of damages proven, plus court cost and attorney fees.
Exceptions	Actions: Single acts are not covered, there must be a (12) _______ of activity.
Other	Definitions: (13) ______________ means any act or threat involving arson, gambling, kidnapping, murder, robbery, bribery, extortion, dealing in obscene matter, or dealing in a controlled substance. A (14) __________ is two or more violations within a ten year period. (15)__________damages are three times the amount of actual damages. Answers: 1. enterprise, 2. racketeering, 3. relatedness, 4. launder, 5. racketeering, 6. conspire, 7. federal and state, 8. one, 9. three, 10. Four, 11. treble, 12. pattern, 13.Racketeering activities, 14. pattern, 15. Treble.

Railway Labor Act (RLA)[29]

Provision	*Description*
Coverage	Organizations: Applies to employers in the railroad and (1) ______ industries, that are engaged in interstate commerce. Individuals: Applies to (2) ________ working in airline industries. Actions: Created the (3) ____________________ to handle disputes between covered employers and labor unions and promoted voluntary bargaining, arbitration and mediation as the best method for resolving the disputes that the board could not settle. Minimizes (4) _______ strikes. The (5) ___________ is the source of the" work now, grieve later" rule.
Regulations	Restrictions: Prohibits employers from discriminating against employees who belong to (6) ____________. Prohibits employees from engaging in (7) _______ and/or lockouts, unless all (8) ___________ routes have been exhausted. Benefits: Covered laborers have the right to form unions. Covered employers are protected from disruptions in (9) _____________. Employers cannot force workers to (10) _____________ through company-controlled unions. Employers cannot require new employees to sign any type of (11) ____________ promising to join or not to join a union. The first step in contract negations where the parties meet without a mediator is called (12) _____________________.
Enforcement	Administration: The (13) ________________________ enforces the RLA, conducts union representational (14) ____________, and supervises the mediation of (15) _________ negotiations. The National Mediation Board is appointed by the President. They can prevent interruptions in commerce for up to (16) ______ days. The three members can have no ties to the (17) __________ industry and one of the members must be of a different political party than the current President. Their term of office is three years. Timing: (18) ____________ bargaining agreements under the RLA have (19) ________ dates, rather than expiration dates. Contracts continue to be in effect until both parties agree on changes. The union and the company have the legal obligation to maintain the (20) __________ until the process has been completed. If all mediation efforts have been exhausted, there is a (21) ____day cooling- off

	period. Near the end of the cooling off period, the mediator will call the parties back. If an agreement is still not reached, parties may engage in (22) ________. If the mediator feels that the dispute cannot be resolved and commerce will be seriously interrupted, the President can create the (23) _______________ Board. The Board has about 30 days to provide reasonable proposals. There is another 30 day cooling off period after proposal delivery. During (24) _________, the National Mediation Board has the authority to say when the two parties will meet. Penalties: Employees have the right to sue their employers if there has been a violation.
Exceptions	Organizations: Trucking services owned and operated by RLA-covered employers are not covered by the Act.
Documents	Records: Employers and unions must submit (25)__________ notices to the other party (26)_____ day(s) in advance of contract changes made in rates of pay, work (27)_______, or (28)______ . The Mediation Board must make an annual report to Congress. Posters: The mediation board will notify the carrier where the printed notice will be posted stating that all disputes will be handled in accordance with act requirements.
Other	Definitions: (29) ________________________ are contracts under which employers and union employees operate. (30)________ is anything an employer or union does to serve its own economic interests, such as hiring replacement workers, or striking. (31)_____________ are advance notices that a party intends to change the terms of the agreement. Answers: 1. airline, 2. employees, 3. National Mediation Board, 4. wildcat, 5. Railway Labor Act, 6. unions, 7. strikes, 8. mediation, 9. commerce, 10. bargain, 11. contract, 12. direct negotiations, 13. National Mediation Board, 14. elections, 15. contract, 16. 60, 17. railway or airline, 18. collective, 19. amenable, 20. status quo, 21. 30, 22. self-help, 23. Presidential Emergency, 24. mediation, 25. Section Six, 26. 30, 27. rules, 28. conditions, 29. Collective bargaining agreements, 30. Self-help, 31. Section Six notices.

Rehabilitation Act of 1973[30]

Provision	*Description*
Coverage	Organizations: Applies to employers with federal (1) _______ and/or sub-contracts that exceed (2) _______ must take reasonable steps to (3) _______, retain, and promote qualified individuals with disabilities. Individuals: Applies to employees and applicants who have a disability to employers with federal contracts.
Regulations	Restrictions: Covered employers must take affirmative steps to employ qualified individuals with disabilities who can perform (4) _________ functions with reasonable (5) __________ without (6) ________ hardship to the covered organization. This applies to all employment and personnel practices such as recruitment, hiring, rates of pay, upgrading, and selection for training. Benefits: Prohibits (7) ________________ in employment against qualified individuals with disabilities. Contractors must make all efforts to use outreach (8) ____________ to hire and advance qualified disabled individuals.
Enforcement	Administration: The Act is enforced by the (9) ______________________________ (OFCCP). The standards for determining discrimination are the same as the Americans with Disabilities Act. Employees and applicants have the right to file a (10) __________ with OFCCP if they feel they have been (11) ______________ against on the basis of disability. Timing: Complaints must be filed within (12) _______ days of a violation unless the filing is extended for a good cause. Extensions must be approved by the OFCCP's Deputy Assistant Secretary. If a complaint is filed against a contractor, he or she has (13) _____ days to request a review by an Administrative Law Judge. Appeals can be taken to the (14) ____________________. Penalties: Employers in violation of the act may have to provide equitable (15) ______ to the victim(s) of discrimination. In some cases, violations will result in (16) _____________, termination, or suspension of federal contracts.
Exceptions	Organizations: (17) ________________ performing work outside of the U.S, contracts not exceeding $10,000, for work that is performed out the U.S. and for contracts with state or local governments. If it is found that the contract is essential to national security then waivers may be granted for noncompliance with the act.

	Individuals: Individuals without disabilities, drug addicts and (18) ________ not in approved treatment programs, gamblers, and individuals with minor or temporary problems, such as a broken bone. Actions: Some cases may prove to cause (19) ___________ hardship to employers.
Documents	A (20) ________________________must be prepared and maintained when a government contractor has 50 or more employees and a contract of $50,000 or more. The program must be reviewed (21) ______________ and must be available for employees and applicants to review. All covered contractors and subcontractors must include a specific (22) ______________________ clause in each of their non-exempt contracts.
Other	Definitions: (23) ___________are physical or mental impairment that constitutes or results in a substantial impediment to employment or substantially limits one or more major life activities. (24)________________are those tasks that are reasonably necessary to do the job. (25)____________ is any action that is so financially large as to disrupt company operations. (26)__________________________ are disabled people who can do the essential job functions with reasonable accommodations. Answers: 1. contracts, 2. $10,000, 3. hire, 4. essential job, 5. accommodation, 6. undue, 7. discrimination, 8. Employment practices, 9. Office of Federal Contract Compliance Programs, 10. complaint, 11. discriminated, 12. 300, 13. 20, 14. Department of Labor Administrative Review Board, 15. relief, 16. cancellation, 17. Federal contractors, 18. alcoholics, 19. undue, 20. affirmative action program, 21. Annually, 22. equal opportunity, 23. Disabilities, 24. Essential job functions, 25. Undue hardship, 26. Qualified individuals with disabilities.

Retirement Equity Act of 1984 (REA)[31]

Provision	*Description*
Coverage	Organizations: Applies to most private sector employers offering (1) __________ benefit plans. Individuals: Applies to all (2) _______ employee benefit plan participants who are (3) _____________ in the plan, their spouses, and beneficiaries. Actions: Covers pension and (4) _______________ benefit plans.
Regulations	Benefits: Reduces the (5) ________ age that an employer may require for participation in a pension plan, (6) __________ the period of time a participant could be absent for work without losing pension credits, and created spousal rights to pension benefits through (7) ________________________ (QDROs).
Enforcement	Administration: The (8) __________________________ (EBSA) under the Department of Labor enforces the Act. Penalties: A fine of up to (9) _____ per calendar year in which a plan administrator fails to provide notice.
Exceptions	Organizations: The Act does not cover plans maintained by governmental entities, (10) _______, or plans that are only established to comply with applicable worker's compensation, unemployment or disability laws.
Documents	Records: Administrators of employee benefit plans are required to give participants and beneficiaries a (11) ______________ description including their rights, benefits, and responsibilities.
Other	Definitions: When (12) ___________, a participant has a right to retirement benefits that cannot be denied. A (13)_________________________ is a court order that provides specialized instructions to plan administrators as to how to pay a divorced spouse, child, or other dependent all or a portion of a pension. Answers: 1. employee, 2. married, 3. vested, 4. welfare, 5. maximum, 6. lengthened, 7. Qualified Domestic Relations Orders, 8. Employee Benefits Security Administration, 9. $5,000, 10. churches, 11. summary plan, 12. vested, 13. Qualified Domestic Relation Order.

Revenue Reconciliation Act of 1993 (RRA)[32]

Provision	*Description*
Coverage	Organizations: Applies to all businesses subject to (1) _________. Individuals: Applies to all individuals subject to income tax, especially those with high annual (2) __________. Actions: Involves the adjusted tax (3) ____________ for individuals and corporations falling within the guidelines.
Regulations	Restrictions: Changes the tax code regarding tax brackets and (4) ___________. Benefits: Proposes to reduce the (5) ______________.
Enforcement	Administration: The Act is enforced by the (6) __________________. Penalties: Tax (7) ______ can result in civil or criminal lawsuits that can force repayment or other punishments.
Exceptions	Organizations: Does not apply to corporations with taxable income less than (8) _____ million. Individuals: Does not apply to joint filers with taxable income less than (9) ______ or individuals with taxable incomes less than (10) ______.
Documents	Records: Submission of income tax return forms is required for corporations and individuals. For individuals, W-2 forms from employers are proof of income and must be attached to form 1040.
Other	Definitions: (11) _________ is the result of subtracting all allowable deductions as set forth in tax laws from gross income. (12)____________ are married persons filing tax returns on combined income. (13)_________________________ are reduction of taxable income equal to the value of donations to charities by a person. (14)_________ is when and individual, corporation, trust, or other entity unlawfully avoids paying taxes. Answers: 1. income tax, 2. incomes, 3. brackets, 4. deductions, 5. federal deficit, 6. Internal Revenue Service (IRS), 7. evasion, 8. $10, 9. $140,000, 10. $115,000, 11. Taxable income, 12. Joint Filers, 13. Charitable contribution deductions, 14. Tax evasion.

Sarbanes-Oxley Act of 2002 (SOX)[33]

Provision	*Description*
Coverage	Organizations: Applies to any (1) ___________ company under the jurisdiction of the (2) ________________. Individuals: Applies to any (3) ________, employee, contractor, subcontractor, or agent of a covered company. Actions: Limits the actions and services of independent (4) ________ and corporate officers. Requires the certification of (5) ___________ statements by top executives.
Regulations	Restrictions: Bans (6) ________ loans to any executive officer or director. Credit can be offered to executive officers if the same offer is offered to the general public. Prohibits insider trades during pension fund (7) _______ periods. REPORTING: Requires reporting of Chief Executive Officer (CEO) and Chief Financial Officer (CFO) (8) __________. Requires auditor (9) ____________, and prohibits certain actions and services by auditors. Requires independent annual reports on the existence and condition of internal financial reporting controls. SECURITIES AND EXCHANGE COMMISSION (SEC): The SEC has (10) _______________ over the (11) _________________________________Board (PCAOB). The board must file proposed rules and changes with the SEC. Any sanctions issued by the board must are reviewed by the SEC. Any rulings made by the board may be overturned by the SEC. All public accounting firms must (12) __________ with the board if they will be auditing public companies. The SEC or the board my order an inspection of a firm at any time. (13)__________reviews for firms that audit more than 100 issues otherwise the review is each three years. DOCUMENTATION: The board must have audit standards that occur in accordance with (14) ____________________ (GAAP) and must record any weaknesses noted in internal controls. All documentation the board has in (15) __________ and can only be released during pubic proceedings or for certain disciplinary actions.

	The SEC has the right to bar or deny any person the right to practice before the SEC if they do not have the (16)__________ or have knowingly violated (17)__________ and can prohibit anyone convicted or securities fraud for being an officer or director of any publicly traded company. The (18) ________________ of a company must certify that all financial documents filed with the SEC meet all provisions of the securities and exchange act. Benefits: Creates the (19) ______________________ (PCAOB) as an accounting oversight board. Provides protection to (20) ______ by improving the accuracy and reliability of corporate disclosures made pursuant to securities laws. Provides (21) __________ protection for employees assisting in investigation of fraud or other conduct.
Enforcement	Administration: Oversight is by (22) __________, and enforcement by the (23) ________________. The board has five members who are appointed for terms of five years. Three of the five cannot have been Certified Public Accountants (CPAs). The other two must be CPAs or at some point in the past been CPAs. Penalties: Fines of up to (24) ______ million for corporations, and (25) _____ for individuals or a maximum of (26) ______ years of imprisonment. The SEC has the authority to bar any person who they deem to have violated the act from acting as an officer or director.
Exceptions	Organizations: Does not apply to (27) __________ companies.
Documents	Records: Audit work papers must be retained for (28) _______ year(s). Financial reports that are prepared in accordance with GAAP must show all correcting adjustments and the SEC will determine if generally accepted accounting rules were used.
Other	Definitions: An (29) __________ is the examination of financial statements of the organization by an independent accounting firm. Answers: 1. publicly-traded, 2. Securities and Exchange Commission (SEC), 3. officer, 4. auditors, 5. financial, 6. personal, 7. blackout, 8. compensation, 9. independence, 10. authority, 11. Public Company Accounting Standards, 12. register, 13. Annual, 14. Generally Accepted Accounting Standards, 15. confidential, 16. qualifications, 17. federal securities

	law, 18. CEO and CFO, 19. Public Company Accounting Oversight Board, 20. investors, 21. whistleblower, 22. PCAOB, 23. Securities and Exchange Commission, 24. $25, 25. $250,000, 26. 25, 27. Private, 28. 7, 29. audit.

Service Contract Act of 1965 (SCA)[34]

Provision	*Description*
Coverage	Organizations: Applies to any contractor or (1) __________ performing work on (2) _______ contracts within the United States and District of Columbia, whose value exceeds (3) _____. Individuals: Applies to (4) _______ employees working under covered contracts. Actions: Applies to (5) __________ determinations.
Regulations	Restrictions: Requires contractors to pay covered employees the locally (6) ________ wage, and requires that covered employees be in (7) ____ working conditions.
Enforcement	Administration: The (8) _____________ division of the Department of Labor enforces the wage provisions of this Act. (9) ________________ enforces the safety and health provisions within the Act. Penalties: Funds may be withheld or legally recovered to disperse to employee who were (10) __________. Non-conforming contractors may be debarred from further contract consideration for up to (11) _____ year(s).
Exceptions	Organizations: Contractors whose contracts also fall under the (12) __________ Act, Walsh-Healy Act, and the Communications Act. Individuals: Non-service employees such as bona fide (13) _________, professional, and administrative employees.
Documents	Records: Employment records must be held for (14) _____ year(s) after the completion of the contract. Posters: Notices of this Act must be conspicuously posted.
Other	Answers: 1. subcontractor, 2. federal, 3. $2,500, 4. Service, 5. wage, 6. prevailing, 7. safe, 8. Wage & Hour, 9. OSHA, 10. underpaid, 11. 3, 12. Davis-Bacon, 13. executives, 14. three.

Smith Act of 1940[35]

Provision	*Description*
Coverage	Organizations: Applies to any society, group, or assembly of individuals who teach, advocate, affiliate, or encourage the (1) __________ or destruction of any (2) ___________ in the United States. Individuals: Requires registration of all (3) __________ adults living in the United States. Covers individuals who participate in (4) _________, or who knowingly or willfully support these illegal activities.
Regulations	Restrictions: Prohibits the formation of organizations whose purpose is (5) _________ the government within the United States, or to publicly display any written or (6) _______ matter advocating an overthrow. Established penalties for (7) ____________ within the United States who are unregistered (8) ____________.
Enforcement	Administration: This criminal law is covered by the appropriate law enforcement agencies. Penalties: If (9) ______ or more persons commit any offense under the Act, each may be subject to fines not to exceed (10) _______, imprisonment not to exceed (11) _______ year(s), and will be ineligible for employment by the U.S. government or any agency for the (12) ______ year(s) following the conviction.
Documents	Records: All aliens living within the United States must be registered.
Other	Definitions: (13) _________________ are used to show refusal to accept authority, such as protests or attempts to destroy established authority. Answers: 1. overthrow, 2. government, 3. non-citizen, 4. insurrections, 5. overthrow, 6. printed, 7. aliens, 8. fingerprinted, 9. 2, 10. $10,000, 11. 20, 12. 5, 13. Insurrectionary activities.

Vietnam Era Veteran's Readjustment Assistance Act of 1974 (VEVRAA)[36]

Provision	*Description*
Coverage	Organizations: Applies to employers with (1) ___________ contracts or subcontracts of (2) ______ or more. Individuals: Applies to qualified (3) _______ veterans, Vietnam era (4) _______, special disabled veterans, and veterans who served on (5) _________ during a war or in a campaign or expedition for which a campaign badge has been authorized. Actions: Applies to all employment status decisions.
Regulations	Restrictions: Covered contractors and subcontractors must take (6) _________ steps to employ qualified and covered Vietnam era veterans. Contractors must list job openings with the local office of the State (7) __________ Service. Contractors must make (8) _________ accommodations for physical and mental disabilities of qualified individuals, as long as such accommodations do not cause (9) _____________ on the employer. Prohibits (10) ________________ against employees and applicants who are qualified Vietnam era veterans. Benefits: Veterans preference is employed in hiring veterans for Federal positions. This applies to (11) _______________ and those who served on active duty. This applies to almost all Federal job and also means that a veteran will retain their job during a reduction in force. The Act also covers (12) ________________ in the workplace on the basis of military stature and failure to provide reasonable accommodations.
Enforcement	Administration: This Act is enforced by the (13) ____________________________ (OFCCP), and the (14) ___________________ of the Department of Labor. If any covered veteran believes a contractor of the United States has failed to (15) _________ or refuses to comply with contract provisions relating to veteran employment, the veteran may file a complaint with the OFCCP. Timing: All complaints should be filed no later than (16) _____ days from the date of the alleged violation. Penalties: If a covered veteran feels that a Federal contractor refuses to comply with veteran hiring practices, he may file a complaint with the OFCCP. Employers in violation of the act may have to provide equitable (17) _____ to

	the victim(s) of discrimination. Violations may result in (18) ____________ of federal contracts.
Exceptions	Organizations: Exceptions exist for Federal contractors working outside the U.S. and on contracts worth less than $25,000. When contractors are listing jobs with the (19)___________, they do not have to include job openings for executive and top level management positions that are going to be filled from within the contractors organization or for jobs that are to last three days or less. Individuals: Exceptions exist for Vietnam era veterans that received a (20) ________ discharge.
Documents	Records: Federal contractors must keep (21) _________ related to two years employment from the initial record date. Records only kept for one year if companies have less than 150 employees and if contract is less than $150,000. Federal contractors and sub-contractors must (22) __________ report about the number of employed Vietnam era veterans employed, disabled veterans, and any other protected veterans employed during the year. This applies only to contracts that started before December 1, 2003 and were more than $25,000.
Other	Definitions: (23) ___________________ means a disabled veteran who is capable of performing a particular job, with reasonable accommodation to his or her disability. (24)______________ is a person who served on active duty for more than 180 days, any part of which occurred between August 5, 1964 and May 7, 1975, and was discharged or released with other than a dishonorable discharge; was discharged or released from active duty for a service connected disability if any part was performed between August 5, 1964 and May 7, 1975; or served on active duty for more than 180 days and served in Vietnam between February 28, 1961 and May 7, 1975. (25)______________________ is a person who is entitled to compensation under laws administered by the Department of Veterans Affairs for a disability rated at 30 percent or more. Also, the person also is entitled if he or she is rated at 10 or 20 percent if a serious employment disability has been determined. Another case applies if a person was discharged or released from active duty because of a service-connected disability. Answers: 1. contracts, 2. $25,000, 3. disabled, 4. veterans, 5. active duty, 6. affirmative, 7. employment,

	8. reasonable, 9. undue hardship, 10. discrimination, 11. disabled veterans, 12. harassment, 13. Office of Federal Contract Compliance Programs, 14. Veteran's Employment Service, 15. comply, 16. 180, 17. relief, 18. cancellation, 19. local state unemployment service, 20. dishonorable, 21. records, 22. annually, 23. Qualified disabled veteran, 24. Vietnam era veteran, 25. Special disabled veteran.

Walsh-Healey Public Contracts Act of 1936 (PCA)[37]

Provision	*Description*
Coverage	Organizations: Applies to (1) __________ entering contracts whose value exceeds (2) ________ for the manufacture or furnishing of goods to the U.S. government, its agencies, departments, the District of Colombia, or any corporation whose stock is beneficially owned by the United States. Individuals: Applies to all covered contractor (3) ___________ directly involved with the manufacture of goods. Handicapped home workers who are clients of sheltered workshops are covered.
Regulations	Restrictions: Stipulates that all covered employees must be paid (4) _________ wage, and (5) _________ for all hours worked in excess of 40 hours per week. Prohibits the employment of individuals under the age of (6) ____, and the use of (7) ________ labor. Requires sanitary, safe, and (8) ______________ working conditions. This is administered by OSHA. Holds contractors liable for (9) _______________ actions and violations. Benefits: Provides covered employees with fair wages and working conditions.
Enforcement	Administration: Regulations relating to wages, overtime, and labor are enforced by the (10) ______________ division of the Department of Labor. (11)_____________ enforces those regulations covering the health and safety of employees. Employers who want to pay a special lower rate for disabled workers must apply for a special certificate from the department of labor. Penalties: Fines of (12) ___ per day per employee who is underage or a convict can be assessed. Legal action may be taken by the DOL to collect wage (13) _____________ and fines. Willful violations may result in (14) ____________ of the current contract and a (15) _____ year ban on future contracts. If a contract is cancelled, the original contractor may be liable for contract completion costs. If a contractor has been found guilty, he or she may appeal the decision through the Administrative Review Board.
Exceptions	Organizations: Employers whose goods are purchased by the federal government on the (16) ___________, without a contract, or with a contract not exceeding $10,000 in worth are not covered. Contracts for public utility services including some transportation and communication services are not covered.

	Individuals: Office, custodial, executive, professional, and outside sales employees are not covered. A special (17) _______________ may be paid to (18) ___________, student learners, and disabled workers, if the employer has obtained a special certificate. Employees that are paroled, pardoned, released from (19) ______, or participating in a (20) ______________ program are not covered.
Documents	Records: Basic employment records must be kept for (21) _____ years. Employment records for those directly tied to a contract must be kept for (22) _____ years. OSHA related records must be kept for (23) _____ years. Posters: (24) ____________________ posters on employee rights on government contracts and wage determinations must be conspicuously posted.
Other	Answers: 1. Contractors, 2. $10,000, 3. employees, 4. minimum, 5. overtime, 6. 16, 7. convict, 8. non-hazardous, 9. subcontractor's, 10. Wage & Hour, 11. OSHA, 12. $10, 13. underpayments, 14. cancellation, 15. 3, 16. open-market, 17. minimum wage, 18. apprentices, 19. prison, 20. work-release, 21. 2, 22. 3, 23. 5, 24. Department of Labor.

Worker Adjustment and Retraining Notification Act (WARN)[38]

Provision	*Description*
Coverage	Organizations: Applies to employers with (1) ___ or more employees, excluding those who have worked less than (2) _____ month(s) in the last 12 months, and those working less than an average (3) _____ hour(s) a week. Individuals: Applies to hourly and (4) ______ workers, managerial and supervisory employees. Applies to workers who are terminated from their employment for reasons other than a voluntary quit, retirement, or for cause. Applies to workers who are laid off for more than (5) ______ months or if the work hours reduced by more than ½ each month for at least six months. Actions: Applies to plant (6) ________ and mass (7) _____________.
Regulations	Restrictions: Employers must provide (8) ___ days(s) notice for plant closings that affect less than (9) ____ or more covered employees, and mass layoffs affecting (10) ____ or more employees, or (11) ____ percent of the total workforce. Notice of the closing should be given to the State Rapid Response Dislocated Worker Unit, the (12) _______ union and to the (13) ________ government which government that the employer paid the most taxes to. In companies that have (14) _________________ the employer should try to notify the employee who will lose his or her job due to bumping. Employers must give notice if they have a series of (15) ______ layoffs which would cause them to fall under the Act. Notices for plant closings or layoffs must be in (16) _______ and be formal. Verbal notices, notices in the newspaper, and paycheck notices do not fall under the Act requirements. Benefits: The act provides assistance to affected workers, their families and communities through the (17) _______________________. This encompasses job search, placement assistance, on-the-job training, classroom training, or additional upper level education to complete a degree,
Enforcement	Administration: The Act is enforced through the United States' (18) ____________________________________. Individual or class action suits may be brought to court and reasonable attorney fees may be part of the cost to the company.

	Timing: Notices must be posted at least (19) _____ days prior to plant closings or mass layoffs. Additional notice must be given if the plant closing is extended beyond the date on the original notice. Or if it does not fit into the (20) ______ window that they have identified as the closing date. Penalties: Employers who fail to comply with the Act may be liable for back pay and benefits to each affected employee. A civil penalty not to exceed (21) ____ per day may also be assessed.
Exceptions	Organizations: Employers do not have to give notice if the plant closing or mass layoff occurs at a (22) __________ facility, or at the end of a (23) _____. Employers also do not have to give notice if work hours are not reduced more than 50% in each month of six months. Individuals: Exceptions include business partners, (24) __________ (workers out on a labor dispute), temporary workers, and local, state, and federal employees. No notices need to be provided to employees who are terminated for just cause, retired, resigned, or transferred to a job with a reasonable commute. Actions: Notices are not required under three exceptions: (25) ___________ business circumstances, natural disasters, and (26) _________. Written notices to employees do not apply if the company is (27) ____________ represented. In this case the union is notified within the 60 day time-frame and they have the option when to notify the employees.
Documents	All notices about the plant closing must be in writing and received 60 days before the closing. Notices must inform employees if the closing affects all or part of the plant, whether the closing is permanent and whether there are bumping rights. The names and phone numbers of the persons to contact for more information also should be provided.
Other	Definitions: (28) __________________________ occur when a company could not have reasonably foreseen the closings or layoffs within their company. A (29) ______________ is a company that is seeking new capital to continue operations, and the reporting of layoffs and closings would negatively affect their ability to obtain the capital. Answers: 1. 100, 2. six, 3. twenty, 4. salary, 5. six, 6. closings, 7. mass layoffs, 8. sixty, 9. fifty, 10. five hundred,

	11. thirty-three, 12. local, 13. local, 14. bumping rights, 15. small, 16. writing, 17. State Rapid Response Dislocated Worker's Unit, 18. district courts, 19. 60, 20. 14 day, 21. $500, 22. temporary, 23. project, 24. strikers, 25. unforeseeable, 26. faltering company, 27 union, 28. Unforeseeable business circumstances, 29. Faltering company.

Endnotes

1. Equal Employment Opportunity Commission. "Civil Rights Act of 1964." http://www.eeoc.gov/laws/statutes/titlevii.cfm (accessed January 12, 2014).

2. Department of Labor. "Youth and Labor." http://www.dol.gov/dol/topic/youthlabor/ (accessed January 12, 2014).

3. Equal Employment Opportunity Commission. "Civil Rights Act of 1964." http://www.eeoc.gov/laws/statutes/titlevii.cfm (accessed January 12, 2014).

4. Equal Employment Opportunity Commission. "Civil Rights Act of 1991." http://www.eeoc.gov/laws/statutes/cra-1991.cfm (accessed January 12, 2014).

5. Department of Labor. "Consolidated Omnibus Budget Reconciliation Act." http://www.dol.gov/dol/topic/health-plans/cobra.htm (accessed January 12, 2014).

6. Department of Labor. "Consumer Credit Protection Act." http://www.dol.gov/compliance/laws/comp-ccpa.htm (accessed January 12, 2014).

7. Department of Labor. "Davis-Bacon Act." http://www.dol.gov/whd/govcontracts/dbra.htm (accessed January 12, 2014).

8. Internal Revenue Service, "Deficit Reduction Act of 1984." http://www.irs.gov/pub/irs-tege/eotopica85.pdf (Accessed January 28, 2014)

9. Department of Labor. "Employee Polygraph Protection Act." http://www.dol.gov/compliance/laws/comp-eppa.htm (accessed January 12, 2014).

10. Equal Employment Opportunity Commission (2014). "Equal Pay Act." http://www.eeoc.gov/laws/statutes/epa.cfm (accessed January 12, 2014).

11. Cornell Law School. "Fair Credit and Reporting Act." http://www.law.cornell.edu/uscode/text/15/chapter-41/subchapter-III (accessed January 12, 2014).

12. Department of Labor, "Fair Labor Standards Act." http://www.dol.gov/compliance/laws/comp-flsa.htm (accessed January 12, 2014).

13. Department of Labor. "Family Medical Leave Act." http://www.dol.gov/whd/fmla/ (accessed January 12, 2014).

14. Cornell Law School. "Federal Insurance Contribution Act." http://www.law.cornell.edu/uscode/text/26/subtitle-C/chapter-21 (accessed January 12, 2014).

15. Internal Revenue Service. Federal Unemployment Tax Act, http://www.irs.gov/Individuals/International-Taxpayers/Federal-Unemployment-Tax (accessed January 12, 2014).

16. Department of Labor. "Health Insurance Portability and Accountability Act." http://www.dol.gov/ebsa/newsroom/fshipaa.html (accessed January 12, 2014).

17. Cornell Law School. "Health Maintenance Organization Act." http://

www.law.cornell.edu/uscode/text/42/300e (accessed January 12, 2014).

18. Department of Labor. "Immigration Reform and Control Act." http://www.dol.gov/ofccp/regs/compliance/ca_irca.htm (accessed Jan-uary 12, 2014).

19. Department of Labor. "Landrum Griffin Act." http://www.dol.gov/compliance/laws/comp-lmrda.htm (accessed January 12, 2014).

20. Department of Labor. "Mental Health Parity Act." Retrieved from http://www.dol.gov/ebsa/mentalhealthparity/ (accessed January 12, 2014).

21. Cornell Law School. "Military Selective Service Act." http://www.law.cornell.edu/uscode/html/uscode50a/usc_sup_05_50_10_sq8.html (accessed January 12, 2014).

22. Cornell Law School. "Norris LaGuardia Act." http://www.law.cornell.edu/uscode/text/29/107 (accessed January 12, 2014).

23. Department of Labor. "Occupational Safety and Health Act." http://www.dol.gov/compliance/laws/comp-osha.htm (accessed January 12, 2014).

24. Department of Labor. "Patient Protection and Affordable Care Act." http://www.dol.gov/ebsa/healthreform/ (accessed January 12, 2014).

25. Cornell Law School. "Postal Reorganization Act." http://www.law.cornell.edu/uscode/text/39/101 (accessed January 12, 2014).

26. Equal Employment Opportunity Commission. "Pregnancy Discrimination Act." http://www.eeoc.gov/laws/statutes/pregnancy.cfm (accessed January 12, 2014).

27. Justice Department. "Privacy Act." http://www.justice.gov/opcl/privstat.htm (accessed January 12, 2014).

28. Cornell Law School. "Racketeer Influenced and Corrupt Organ-ization Act." http://www.law.cornell.edu/uscode/text/18/part-I/chapter-96 (accessed January 12, 2014).

29. National Mediation Board. "Railway Labor Act." http://www.nmb.gov/documents/rla.html (accessed January 12, 2014).

30. Department of Labor. "Rehabilitation Act." http://www.dol.gov/oasam/regs/statutes/sec504.htm (accessed January 12, 2014).

31. Internal Revenue Service. "Retirement Equity Act." http://www.irs.gov/irm/part4/irm_04-072-009.html (accessed January 12, 2014).

32. Taxprophet.com. "Revenue Reconciliation Act." http://www.taxprophet.com/archives/pubs/rra_nl.html (accessed January 12, 2014).

33. U. S. Government Printing Office. "Sarbanes Oxley Act." http://www.gpo.gov/fdsys/pkg/PLAW-107publ204/html/PLAW-107publ204.htm (accessed January 12, 2014).

34. Department of Labor, "Service Contract Act of 1964." http://www.dol.gov/oasam/regs/statutes/351.htm (accessed January 12, 2014).

35. Boston College. "Smith Act." www.bc.edu/bc_org/avp/cas/comm/free_speech/smithactof1940.html (accessed January 12, 2014).

36. Department of Labor. "Vietnam Era Veterans Readjustment Assistance Act." http://www.dol.gov/compliance/laws/comp-vevraa.htm (accessed January 12, 2014).

37. Department of Labor. "Walsh Healey Public Contracts Act." http://

www.dol.gov/compliance/laws/comp-pca.htm (accessed January 12, 2014).

38. Department of Labor. "Worker Adjustment and Retraining Notification Act." http://www.dol.gov/compliance/laws/comp-warn.htm (accessed January 12, 2014).

Chapter Six

Multiple Choice

PURPOSE

To help students study for the human resource certification exams. Answer key is in the back of the chapter.

WAYS TO PLAY

Test Simulation

One player: Answer the questions and then check the answer sheet at the back of the test. This is rocket science.

Two or More Players: Answer a section such as "Strategy" and see who gets a higher score.

Grab Clues

Two or more players: Have one person state a question and have another try to answer it. Take turns. If that person knows it, he or she should answer it. If he or she does not don't know it, then pick from clues set before the game started. Only one type of clue can be used per game. Players get one point per right answer and lose one for wrong. The player with the most points wins.

1. Consult this book, HR textbook, dictionary, teammate, or the Internet for one minute.
2. Look at the answer key for 15 seconds.
3. Skip the question and have the next one count double.

Strategy

1. Who sponsors the Assurance of Learning, Professional in Human Resources, and Senior Professional in Human Resources certification exams?
   a. American Society of Personnel Administration
   b. American Compensation and Benefits Association
   c. National Human Resource Specialists
   d. Society for Human Resource Management

2. After a bachelor's degree, how many years of experience is/are required to qualify for a Professional in Human Resource (PHR) exam?
   a. 1
   b. 2
   c. 3
   d. 5

3. Which certification is associated with nine exams—3 general business exams, 3 required in the area, and 3 elective exams?
   a. CBP
   b. CPLP
   c. PHR
   d. EEOC

4. Typical corporate visions look at how long into the future?
   a. 1-2 months
   b. 6 months-1 year
   c. 1-2 years
   d. 3-5 years

5. How should company policies concerning electronic surveillance of employees be written?
   a. General statement should state that the employer is allowed to view any website
   b. Internal corporate communications can be monitored at any time
   c. There is a guarantee that web privacy rights will prevail
   d. Employees are not allowed to write any negative statements associated with the company in any website

6. What is the most team-oriented generation?
   a. Baby boomers
   b. Generation X
   c. Generation Y
   d. Millennium Generation

7. Which of the following is true about comp time?
   a. Comp time must be provided before the next pay day
   b. Comp time can continue indefinitely
   c. Comp time is not increasing due to the economy
   d. Comp time is illegal in the private sector

Employment

8. Frost Corporation has 250 employees in Boise, Idaho and makes trophies. Its application form has the following four statements. Which one is legal?
   a. Desired salary_______________
   b. Polygraph test results_______________
   c. Maiden Name____________________
   d. Type of Military Discharge____________________

9. Tolefson Corporation has 250 employees in Waco, Texas and makes stringed instruments. Its application form as the following four questions. Which one is legal?
   a. Have you ever had cancer?
   b. Are you gay or lesbian?
   c. When did you graduate high school?
   d. How many pounds can you lift?

10. Jelema Company has 250 employees in Cape Coral, Florida and makes decorative flags. Its application form has the following four questions. Which one is legal?
    a. Have you ever been arrested?
    b. Have you ever been convicted?
    c. Have you ever had a garnishment?
    d. Have you ever made decorative flags?

11. Weinbrenner Company has 15 employees in Mobile, Alabama. Alabama discrimination laws are not stricter than national discrimination laws. Weinbrenner's application form has the following four questions. Which one is legal?
    a. What is your age?
    b. What is your gender?
    c. What is your race?
    d. What is your national origin?

12. In an application form, companies are not allowed to ask if a person is a member of a union. What labor law is applicable?
    a. Fair Labor Standards Act
    b. Clayton Antitrust Act
    c. National Labor Relations Act
    d. National Industrial Recovery Act

13. Which of the following is a BFOQ?
    a. Recent high school graduates needed to enter Cedar Falls' restaurant management
    b. Flight attendants for Waterloo Airlines must have a minimum height of five feet
    c. Need salesmen to sell Waverly Brushes in the Tri-State area
    d. Need men to clean bathroom stalls at the Wartburg Knights' stadium

14. Which of the following is a case most associated with business necessity?
    a. A male working in a factory in Columbia
    b. A female cleaning a restroom
    c. A black actor
    d. A flight attendant shorter than 5'10"

15. For what size company does the Civil Rights Act of 1964 apply?
    a. 10
    b. 15
    c. 20
    d. 50

16. To make a reasonable accommodations, how should restaurants handle blind customers?
    a. Create Braille menus
    b. Keep such customers out of the restaurant
    c. Provide only select meal items
    d. Have servers read the menu

17. Executive orders tend to apply to what type of organizations?
    a. Government contractors
    b. State and local governments
    c. Private sector companies with 15 or more employees
    d. Private sector companies with 25 or more employees

18. According to McDonnell Douglas vs. Green, who has the second burden of proof in discrimination cases?
    a. Judge
    b. Jury
    c. Defendant
    d. Plaintiff

19. What kind of norming is legal on Federal exams?
    a. Gender
    b. Handicapped
    c. Race
    d. National identity

20. What did the Civil Rights Act of 1991 state?
    a. No quotas
    b. Open adoption of handicap restrictions
    c. Genetic analysis of individuals is legal
    d. Matrix management

21. Which of the following is an undue hardship?
    a. Marge was not hired because she revealed that her old boss was a stupid idiot
    b. Debby was not hired because the observatory on the 4th floor had no wheelchair access for the company with three employees
    c. Kyle was not hired because he was too young to fly a plane
    d. Natalie was not hired because the company decided not to pay for a $10 hearing assist device for the phone

22. Which of the following is a job specification?
    a. Maintains clean office.
    b. Job Title: Building Contractor
    c. Approved By: Amanda Queen
    d. Three years of experience as an electrical technician

23. Which of the following is an essential job function?
    a. High school education or equivalent required
    b. Working conditions: Must sit for extended periods of time
    c. Supervisor: Alexandra Higgins
    d. Flies airplane

24. Which of the following is always an action verb?
    a. Does
    b. Works
    c. Performs
    d. Eliminates

25. In O*NET, what does the details section have that the summary section does not have?
    a. Job specifications
    b. Ratings from 1 to 100
    c. Estimated pay
    d. Job context

26. What is "Performs other tasks as required" otherwise known as?
    a. An elastic clause
    b. A disjoint clause
    c. A modifier
    d. A reverse task

27. Who developed O*NET?
    a. State employment agencies
    b. Civil Service Commission
    c. National Bureau of Statistics
    d. Department of Labor

28. Brookelyn has a problem with the Silver Springs initiative in the company. What is probably the best way to deal with the problem?
    a. Hide the problem
    b. Hire an outside consultant
    c. Train employees to fix the problem
    d. Get commitment from the CEO

29. Which of the following comes first?
    a. Job descriptions
    b. Job evaluations
    c. Job analysis
    d. Performance appraisals

30. What does the Position Analysis Questionnaire focus on?
    a. Tasks
    b. Processes
    c. Work rules
    d. How to do a job

31. What is the number one skill managers should have according to O*NET?
    a. Speaking
    b. Writing
    c. Active listening
    d. Computer skills

32. What is the process of positioning an organization as an employer of choice in the labor market?
    a. Original marketing
    b. Company benchmarking
    c. Employment branding
    d. Target selection

33. With touch point mapping, what does a touch point refer to?
    a. Critical interaction with a candidate
    b. The cost of marketing a job
    c. The spot in the interview process in which the job candidate made the decision to select the job
    d. Big plans

34. What is an example of a long-term metric in recruiting?
    a. Average time required to recruit applicants
    b. Cost per applicant hired
    c. EEO hiring rates
    d. Performance of hires

35. What recruiting tool is most associated with a piece of paper on a door?
    a. Newspaper
    b. Point of contact
    c. Internet
    d. Billboard

36. With what recruiting sources is cheating severely penalized?
    a. Direct mail
    b. Directories
    c. Recruitment services
    d. Billboards

37. Why would a company typically use a billboard to recruit?
    a. Advertise to national audience
    b. Advertise one job to a local market
    c. Advertise several jobs to a local market
    d. Advertise in the regional market

38. What is the most popular career website in the United States?
    a. Dice
    b. Monster
    c. Career builder
    d. LinkedIn

39. Which of the following is for long-term recruiting efforts?
    a. Directories
    b. National newspapers
    c. Local newspapers
    d. Television

40. What must exist with selection testing before anything else is appropriate?
    a. Validity
    b. Adverse impact
    c. Reliability
    d. Utility

41. What type of validity is impractical because we have to hire all who apply?
    a. Construct
    b. Concurrent
    c. Content
    d. Predictive

42. What type of reliability is best if there is a problem of learning from the previous exam?
    a. Parallel
    b. Test-retest
    c. Split half
    d. Even grade

43. What government document provides tips on how to develop accurate and legal selection tests?
    a. Department of Labor Directive
    b. Legal Mindset
    c. Test Clearinghouse
    d. Uniform Guidelines

44. What is associated with unintentional discrimination?
    a. Adverse treatment
    b. Adverse impact
    c. High volume control
    d. Low volume control

45. Women hired 5, Female applicants 20, Men hired 25, Male applicants 50. According to the 80% rule, what can we conclude?
    a. There is no evidence of discrimination against women
    b. There is evidence of discrimination against women
    c. There is evidence of discrimination against men
    d. There is insufficient evidence to make any conclusions

46. When does the 80% rule become statistically absurd?
    a. Low sample size
    b. The best people are hired
    c. Recruiters use web-based performance measures
    d. There are tight deadlines

47. What adverse impact analysis takes into account the number of qualified applicants?
    a. Investment
    b. Assistance
    c. Balanced Design
    d. Utilization

Development

48. What are the three phases of training in the right order?
    a. Training, evaluation, assessment
    b. Evaluation, training, assessment
    c. Assessment, training, evaluation
    d. Assessment, evaluation, training

49. According to andragogy theory, what do adults prefer to avoid?
    a. Focusing on one training method
    b. Hands on activities
    c. Relevance
    d. Participation

50. When teaching on television, what should you do?
    a. Focus only on the audience in front of you
    b. Look at the camera often
    c. Wear all black outfits
    d. Wear all white outfits

51. What is an example of t-groups?
    a. Behavior modeling
    b. Programmed instruction
    c. Research conference
    d. Alcoholics Anonymous

52. During orientation, what would be most appropriate?
    a. Introducing the new employee to many people
    b. Providing the new employee a difficult assignment
    c. Informing the new employee of where the bathrooms are
    d. Letting the new employee take on the job on his/her own without help

53. What group gets unrelated training?
    a. Experimental
    b. Placebo
    c. Control
    d. Trained

54. What is the hardest data to collect concerning training programs according to Kirkpatrick?
    a. Results
    b. Learning
    c. Behavior
    d. Reaction

55. What is the research-based way of doing performance appraisal?
    a. Manager does the appraisal
    b. Rating scales are the instruments used
    c. Appraisals are modified by management opinions
    d. Appraisals are done periodically and negotiated

56. What is an example of a type of essay?
    a. Checklist
    b. BARS
    c. Critical incidents
    d. Ranking

57. What is a phrase that should be in all behaviorally anchored rating scales?
    a. Person is expected to....
    b. Rank the following....
    c. Describe you would do the following....
    d. Find three examples of....

58. What is the problem of having many dimensions on one scale?
    a. Co-factoring
    b. Nonuniformity
    c. Weighting
    d. Multicollinearlty

59. What activity should take the most time in performance appraisals?
    a. Collect documentation
    b. Support grievance rights
    c. Ask structured and open-ended questions in an interview
    d. Follow-up on issues discussed in an interview

60. What is the most effective way to reduce performance appraisal errors?
    a. Benchmark
    b. Perform 360 degree analysis
    c. Have management commitment
    d. Train with clear directions

61. What performance appraisal error involves rating everyone high?
    a. Halo
    b. Leniency
    c. Same as me
    d. Politics

62. What performance appraisal error is similar to order error?
    a. Transcriptional
    b. Sampling
    c. Bias
    d. Contrast

Pay

63. What equity is associated with pay based on seniority, merit, and incentives?
    a. Internal
    b. Strategic
    c. Employee
    d. External

64. When you put together a lead-lag policy, what pay philosophy do you have?
    a. Egalitarian
    b. Leaders get all the spoils
    c. Everyone should be paid above the market
    d. Everyone should be paid below the market

65. What is the most dominant equity in the United States?
    a. Internal
    b. Strategic
    c. Employee
    d. External

66. What is true about pay surveys?
    a. The government survey data is a few weeks old
    b. Most pay analysts at large companies rely on one or two major pay surveys
    c. Government survey data only covers wages and salaries but not benefits
    d. Participating in a private sector survey will often give your company results at half the price

67. What type of pay is above the pay grade due to exceptional merit, seniority, or output?
    a. Monitor levels
    b. Red circle
    c. Screen costs
    d. Project pay

68. What type of job evaluation system is the most common?
    a. Factor comparison
    b. Point
    c. Job classification
    d. Ranking

69. What is the Federal Government's main pay survey?
    a. National Compensation Survey
    b. Personnel Pay Survey
    c. Federal Pay System Survey
    d. United States Pay Track

70. What is a contributing factor that causes pay compression?
    a. Nonoverlapping pay grades
    b. High turnover
    c. Piece rate pay
    d. Inflation

71. What health plan provides the basic benefits and then options that are costed out? There is a budget and employees are to select from the menu.
    a. Core plan
    b. Benefits bank
    c. Alternative dinners
    d. Benefits sequence

72. What organization protects private pension plans?
    a. PBGC
    b. AIPS
    c. SFTI
    d. WNVC

73. Who pays for unemployment compensation?
    a. Employer
    b. Employee
    c. Taxpayer
    d. County government

74. How can you differentiate Preferred Provider Organizations (PPOs) from Health Maintenance Organizations (HMOs)?
    a. PPOs are designed for nonprofits and HMOs are designed for profits
    b. PPOs are not geographically limited and HMOs are
    c. PPOs penalize employees who go to outside-the-plan physicians and HMOs don't penalized employees who go to outside-the-plan physicians
    d. PPOs are designed for public sector institutions and HMOs are designed for private sector institution

75. What law governs private (defined benefit) pension plans?
    a. COBRA
    b. ERISA
    c. SIMPLEX
    d. HIPAA

76. Highly compensated employees (HCEs) are normally associated with what top percentage of the company?
    a. 1
    b. 2
    c. 3
    d. 4

77. What act places restrictions on the use and disclosure of protected health information?
    a. COBRA
    b. ERISA
    c. SIMPLEX
    d. HIPAA

78. Which of the following is true about the Affordable Care Act?
    a. Individuals can be denied coverage for preexisting conditions
    b. Doctor's income is based on quantity rather than quality
    c. Insurers may increase premiums for profit
    d. Children under the age of 26 can stay on their parent's insurance

Relations

79. What is not part of the hot stove rule?
    a. Immediate
    b. Valid
    c. Consistent
    d. Warning

80. What is the third step in progressive discipline?
    a. Oral warning
    b. Suspension
    c. Discharge
    d. Written warning

81. What is the number one way companies deal with alcohol problems?
    a. Discipline short of discharge
    b. Discharge
    c. In-house counseling
    d. Outside sources

82. What is the most common way companies deal with major employee emotional problems?
    a. Discipline short of discharge
    b. Discharge
    c. In-house counseling
    d. Outside sources

83. What type of discipline is involved when in-house counseling and outside sources are used?
    a. Corrective discipline
    b. Constructive discipline
    c. Destructive discipline
    d. Overt discipline

84. What employee handbook policy could cause a problem with the implied contract exception to employment-at-will?
    a. Specific privacy policies concerning monitoring of company computers
    b. A provision stating that employees have a right never to join a union
    c. Employees can be permanent or temporary
    d. Employees can be full-time or part-time

85. What type of employee handbooks would be associated with the French constitutional style?
    a. Short and general
    b. Long and detailed
    c. Humorous
    d. Irrelevant

86. What is a violation of good faith and fair dealing?
    a. Violating the Civil Rights Act of 1964
    b. Laying off someone shortly after moving him/her to another plant
    c. Firing someone for going on jury duty
    d. Firing someone for whistleblowing

87. What contributed to the Knights of Labor failing?
    a. The use of arbitration rather than strikes
    b. A stronger organization, the Congress of Industrial Organizations, replaced the Knights of Labor
    c. Members were more interested in health care benefits
    d. Injunctions

88. What industry group is NOT covered by the National Labor Relations Act?
    a. Construction
    b. Longshoring
    c. Railroads
    d. Mining

89. What does the Landrum Griffin Act do?
    a. Protects unions from management
    b. Protects management from unions
    c. Protects union members from union leaders
    d. Protects union leaders from union members

90. What type of shop is illegal in all 50 states and is NOT associated with right-to-work legislation?
    a. Union shops
    b. Maintenance of membership shops
    c. Agency shops
    d. Closed shops

91. When did union membership in the United States peak at 33 percent of the working public?
    a. Merger of the AFL and the CIO
    b. World War II
    c. Passage of the Wagner Act
    d. The height of the Knights of Labor

92. How did Republican Senator from Wisconsin Joseph McCarthy help unions in the 1950s?
    a. By helping pass the Wagner Act
    b. By helping kick communists out of unions
    c. By helping pass Civil Rights Acts
    d. By helping negotiate the merger of the AFL and the CIO

93. Which law bans strikes among federal workers?
    a. Civil Service Reform Act
    b. National Labor Relations Act
    c. Norris LaGuardia Act
    d. Walsh Healey Act

94. If you sign a yellow dog contract, what do you promise to do?
    a. Join a union after 30 days
    b. Go on strike
    c. Hire an arbitrator
    d. Never join a union

Health, Safety, and Security

95. Which OSHA form requires companies to write detailed reports of injuries and illnesses?
    a. 300
    b. 300A
    c. 301
    d. 301A

96. From the previous question, how large should a company be before it is required to fill out such form?
    a. 5 employees
    b. 10 employees
    c. 11 employees
    d. 15 employees

97. Who is covered by OSHA?
    a. Trucking companies with 18 employees
    b. Mining companies with 14 employees
    c. Family farms with 3 immediate family members
    d. Independent contractors

98. What is the number on cause of preventable deaths?
    a. Cocaine
    b. Heroin
    c. Smoking
    d. Alcohol

99. Which of the following is recordable to OSHA?
    a. Food poisoning from food brought in by employees to the company
    b. Burns form a personal curling iron
    c. Broken leg from a voluntary pickup company volleyball game
    d. Sprained ankle from a wet floor just inside the company front door after a rainstorm

100. What is the second highest OSHA inspection priority?
   a. Deaths and catastrophes
   b. Immediate danger
   c. Employee complaints
   d. High hazard industries

101. What does a petition for modification of abatement ask for?
   a. A variance
   b. A notice of contest
   c. A warrant
   d. A timing device

102. What is an example of an unsafe condition?
   a. Throwing materials
   b. Making safety devices inoperative by adjusting them
   c. Lifting improperly
   d. Faulty scaffolds

103. What is the total depletion of physical and mental resources caused by trying too hard to reach an unrealistic work-related goal?
   a. Motion disorder
   b. Stress
   c. Burnout
   d. Overtime

104. Who studies and publishes recommendations regarding the use of computer screens, chairs, and other equipment?
   a. Safety First
   b. NIOSH
   c. CDC
   d. MSDS

Answer Key

1. D American Society of Personnel Administration is the predecessor to the Society for Human Resource Management. B and C items do not exist.
2. B One year of experience needed with a masters, two for a bachelors, and four for just a high school diploma.
3. A CBP is a Certified Benefits Professional with the WorldAtWork organization. CPLP is a Certified Professional in Learning and Performance with the American Society for Training and Development.
4. D 3-5 years. Short term objectives are typically less than a year.
5. B Public acknowledgment of monitoring reduces company liability. Statements A, C, and D can increase risk of lawsuits
6. A Baby Boomers tend to focus on the job rather than careers as other generations do. More recent generations tend to be more individualistic.
7. D Compensatory time off is legal in the public sector where it is increasing.
8. A Polygraph test results are a violation of the Polygraph Protection Act. Maiden name violates the Civil Rights Act of 1964. Type of military discharge violates the Americans With Disabilities Act (ADA).
9. B Legal in Texas but not in some other states. Cancer violates ADA. When graduate high school violates Age Discrimination in Employment Act (ADEA). Lifting pounds violates ADA.
10. D Arrests violate the Civil Rights Act of 1964. Genetic testing is a violation of GINA. Garnishments violate the Civil Rights Act of 1964.
11. A Age is legal because the Age Discrimination in Employment Act applies to companies with 20 or more employees. The other items are illegal due to the Civil Rights Act of 1964.
12. C National Labor Relations Act prevents a company from dominating a union even through application forms.
13. D Gender can be used as a Bona Fide Occupational Qualification for the bathroom settings. A violates ADEA. B is a business necessity. C violates the Civil Rights Act of 1964.
14. D Height limits involve safety and business necessity.
15. B But can be much lower if the state law is stronger.
16. D Reading the menu is the easiest and cheapest alternative. Braille menus might be an undue hardship. Other choices may be illegal.
17. A By definition.
18. C Plaintiff first, then defendant, then plaintiff again.
19. B Handicapped individuals get extra points on Federal exams. Veterans also get extra points.

20. A By definition.
21. B Putting wheelchair access to the 4th floor may be an undue hardship on a very small company.
22. D Job specifications can involve experience, education, knowledge, skills, abilities, working conditions
23. D Essential job functions often start with an action verb such as flies, manages, destroys, estimates.
24. D Action verbs always have to say something substantive about the job. "Performs" may work well for acting jobs but not for jobs in general.
25. B By definition.
26. A Elastic clauses stretch the job description to give the job more flexibility.
27. D By definition.
28. D Commitment from the top typically is the most powerful choice. B and C can work. A is counterproductive.
29. C Job analysis is the technical step in HR that precedes everything else.
30. B A process is a general statement such as "Read graphic materials." A task is a specific statement for a job such as "Read blueprints."
31. C Active listening is consistently #1
32. C By definition.
33. A All critical interactions with job candidates need to be analyzed (touchpoint mapped) for their effectiveness.
34. D Performance of hires may looks and them one, two, or more years in the future.
35. B By definition. Point of contact is inexpensive and often for lower level jobs.
36. A Direct mail companies provide addresses that are sent directly back to them to see if individuals sending the mail actually paid for the privilege.
37. C Billboards are typically for a major job marketing effort in the local economy.
38. C By web hits.
39. A Directories tend to stay on people's desks for long periods of time.
40. C Reliability is a prerequisite to proving validity and utility in a selection test.
41. D Predictive validity is impractical but the most statistically sound.
42. A Parallel tests provide similar exams but with different questions the second time. Test-retest provides the same exam twice. Split Half provides different exams at the same time. Even grade does not exist.
43. D By definition. The Uniform Guidelines outline the reliability, validity, and adverse impact analysis for selection tests.
44. B By definition.

45. B The female hiring rate is 50 percent less than the male hiring rate. 50% < 80% so there is evidence for discrimination based on the 80% rule.
46. A Low sample sizes, such as one minority, will lead to either a 0% hiring rate or a 100% hiring rate of minorities compared to the majority group.
47. D Utilization uses hypothesis testing to compare the qualified applicants in the market to what you have in the company.
48. C Assess if you need training and set your objectives, train, and evaluate your training.
49. A Adults like many training methods that are hands on, relevant, and participative.
50. B Looking at the camera increases audience attention. White may be too glaring. Black may make you disappear.
51. D Groups get together to share opinions, feelings.
52. C Employees need the basics and not be avalanched with information.
53. B Experimental=Relevant training, Control=No training.
54. A Reaction is the easiest to collect, then learning, behavior, and results.
55. D Appraisals need to be done regularly but must adapt to the needs of the job.
56. C Critical incidents have performance appraisers write good activities and bad activities that a person has done over a period of time.
57. A For example, person is expected to.....1 arrive 10 minutes late, 2 arrive 5 late, 3 arrive on time, 4 arrive 5 minutes early, 5 arrive 10 minutes early.
58. D Multicollinearity causes problems because multiple dimensions on one scale can make a rater legitimately give a rate two different scores on the same scale.
59. A Documentation should take 99 percent of the time.
60. C Top management commitment to reducing errors has been shown to be typically most effective.
61. B By definition. Halo error involves rating people high based on one characteristic. Leniency involves rating everybody high.
62. D By definition.
63. C Employee equity covers market pay and internal equity covers a comparison of the difficulty of jobs within a company.
64. A People with small paychecks get paid above the market and people with large paychecks get paid below the market.
65. D Market pay dominates.
66. D Just a fact about surveys. Many large companies might use ten or more surveys.
67. B By definition. Green circle is pay below the pay grade. Silver circle is pay above the pay grade due to seniority. Gold circle is pay above the pay grade due to merit.

68. B
69. A Others listed are made up.
70. D Inflation rages while pay for those who stay in the company stays the same. Those who stay fall behind in pay. New hires get paid more.
71. B Core plan has participants chose, for example, 6 of 9 different benefits. Alternative dinners, for example, provide three major groups of benefit choices. Benefits sequence does not exist.
72. A Pension Benefit Guarantee Corporation.
73. A Employer.
74. B By definition.
75. B Employee Retirement Income Security Act.
76. B By definition.
77. D Health Insurance Portability and Accountability Act.
78. D Major feature of the Act.
79. B Hot Stove Rule is a type of discipline mnemonic devise involving providing a warning, and immediate, impersonal, and consistent discipline.
80. B Typical steps in progressive discipline are oral warning, written warning, suspension, and discharge.
81. C In-house counseling
82. D Use of outside sources such as Employee Assistance Programs are often involved.
83. A By definition. Constructive discipline, in contrast, is discipline in which an employer makes life miserable so the employee leaves.
84. C Permanence implies that the employee would be very difficult to fire.
85. B French constitutional style is long and detailed. British common law style (American Constitution) is short and sparse.
86. B Item A is illegal. C and D are a violation of public policy that involves an employee's right as a citizen.
87. D Injunctions forcefully stopped strikes by government order.
88. C Railroads are covered by the Railway Labor Act
89. C Wagner Act protects unions from management. Taft Hartley protects management from unions. Landrum Griffin protects union members from union leaders.
90. D Union shops, maintenance of membership shops, and agency shops are often made illegal by right-to-work laws.
91. A Merger of the AFL-CIO occurred in 1955.
92. B McCarthy was known to be anti-communist.
93. A By definition.
94. D By definition.
95. C Form 300 is the log and summary, 301 is the detailed report, 300A is the annual report, 301A is made up
96. C By law.

97. A Mining companies are covered by Mining Safety and Health Administration. Family farms with three family members are too small. Independent contractors are not involved.
98. B No contest.
99. D Company is responsible for a wet floor. Every other item is a voluntary personal responsibility.
100. A The inspection priorities are 1 Immediate danger, 2 Deaths and catastrophes, 3 Employee complaints, 4 High hazard industries, 5 Follow-up reviews
101. A Variance is an exception to the rules.
102. D Items A, B, and C are unsafe acts
103. B By definition.
104. B By definition. MSDS are Material Safety Data Sheets that describe chemicals and how to handle them. CDC is the Center for Disease Control. Safety First brings safety, technology, and insurance experts together to reduce auto and commercial vehicle collisions.

Epilogue

Studying new human resource materials and content for human resource certifications requires activities that suit your learning style. The Chapter 3 Definition Matrix game provides a contest format that can especially be geared for a group environment. Chapter 4 Brainstorming games allow learners to retrieve a great variety of information about a topic. This is particularly useful when an HR manager confronts a problem and has to think of a wide variety of solutions. Chapter 5 CREEDO provides detailed information about laws in an organized format. Chapter 6 Multiple Choice games look like many certification exam questions so the questions might have high content validity.

What is content validity? Oops, seem to have skipped the term earlier in the book. This validity is the alignment between the training activity (multiple choice questions) and the content or subject area that will be accessed. The multiple choice questions hopefully relate to many of the certification exams listed in Chapter 2.

The games provided in this book are only the "tip of the iceberg" of game possibilities. Many existing games can help create new study games. Go to a toy store or major retail chain and look at various games that require something that resembles a brain to play. Make modifications of the games to create new learning. Go online to read descriptions of various games. An easy method is to type "Types of Games" in any search engine of your choice and find catalogs of interesting games.

Build on the games shown in this book. Each chapter contains several ways to play. Create your own twists. For example, with the Multiple Choice games, if someone does not get an answer correct, force that person to find the correct answer online (within 5 minutes? 10 minutes?). If you get one question right, you get one point. Two consecutive question right are three points (1 +2). Three consecutive questions right are six points (1 + 2 + 3) and so on. Just think of as many game possibilities as you can.

If games are right for you, go for it. If they are not, there are still lots of ways to study that fits your learning style. Reading, discussions, lectures, role plays, online quizzes, online courses, sample tests, and so on may work. Just do what works.

Index